In Schools We Trust

Deborah Meier

In Schools We Trust

Creating Communities of Learning
in an Era of Testing and Standardization

BEACON PRESS | *Boston*

Beacon Press
25 Beacon Street
Boston, Massachusetts 02108-2892
www.beacon.org

Beacon Press books
are published under the auspices of
the Unitarian Universalist Association of Congregations.

Printed in the United States of America

06 05 04 03 02   8 7 6 5 4 3 2 1

This book is printed on acid-free paper that meets the uncoated paper ANSI/NISO
specifications for permanence as revised in 1992.

Composition by Wilsted & Taylor Publishing Services

LIBRARY OF CONGRESS CATALOGING-IN-PUBLICATION DATA
Meier, Deborah.
    In schools we trust : creating communities of learning in an era of testing and
standardization / Deborah Meier.
        p. cm.
Includes bibliographical references.
    ISBN 0-8070-3142-9 (cloth : alk. paper)
    1. Public schools—United States—Case studies. 2. Educational change—United
States—Case studies. 3. Educational tests and measurements—Standards—United
States. I. Title.
    LA217.2 .M44 2002
    371.26'2'0973—dc21
        2001008078

To Vito Peronne,
my friend, colleague, and leader

*I would not lead you to the promised land, because if I could,
others could lead you back again.*
—Eugene V. Debs, 1921

CONTENTS

INTRODUCTION

Five years ago, when I wrote about small schools in East Harlem and what they had to teach the nation's schools, I couldn't have imagined the landscape of education we find ourselves in today. That standardized testing would make a spectacular comeback seemed extremely unlikely. That the majority of states would decide who should be promoted or who should graduate from high school or how much to pay teachers and principals on the basis of standardized test scores seemed far-fetched. That even a conservative federal administration, committed in principle to local control, would mandate annual high-stakes tests for every local schoolhouse in the nation seemed politically impossible. And yet all this has come to pass, and more.

I certainly couldn't have predicted how quickly the lives of schools and kids would be affected by these changes. Schools are increasingly organized around testing, with grave consequences from kindergarten through high school. Children are pressed into earlier and earlier formal literacy activities in order to improve test scores. Learning about the world has been translated, even for four-year-olds, into formats conducive to evaluation by standardized tests. One major city has even outlawed recess in the service of increased desk time. Kids are monitored from morning to nightfall by increasingly undervalued and constrained adults, in highly bureaucratic and powerless institutional settings—and told to keep their noses to the grindstone.

The dominant American attitude toward schooling these days, embodied in all these changes, is a fundamentally new level of distrust. We don't trust teachers' judgment, so we constrain their choices. Nor do we trust principals, parents, or local school boards. We don't trust the public school system as a whole, so we allow those furthest removed from the schoolhouse to dictate policy that fundamentally changes the daily interactions that take place within schools. Nor do we trust in the extraordinary human penchant for learning itself. I believe that this far-reaching distrust has its roots in facts about our lives that go well beyond schooling. There are, after all, good reasons for buyers to beware the goods being sold them, including those that come from their local schools. But whatever the origins, social distrust plays itself out in education in the form of draconian attempts to "restore accountability" through standardized schooling and increasing bureaucratization.

The tragedy of this approach is that it undermines what I think is the best way to make schools trustworthy and raise standards. Standardization and bureaucratization fuel the very distrust they are aimed to cure. Even more tragically, standardization and bureaucratization undermine the possibilities for the kind of education we all claim is sorely lacking. Some of the good news I celebrated five years ago remains good, for sure. Both small schools and public school choice, for example, have increasingly more powerful support in various places. But the larger vision of education those reforms serve is threatened.

This book is about the possibility of a different way to organize our children's schooling. Like some of the proponents of tests and standardization, I too am obsessed by the issue of accountability and adult responsibility for our children. Like them, I believe that the traditional public schools have failed to serve too many people's intellectual needs, including a substantial minority whose children have been dramatically abandoned to unworkable schools. But I believe that the solution lies in the opposite direction. Schools are asked to achieve an extraordinary and revolutionary goal—to provide all children with the kind of schooling once offered only to a small elite—but they are being forced to continue working within factory-style models of schooling and accountability that not only work against that goal but, as I argue, make it impossible. The issue of trust needs to be tackled head-on if we are to embrace this expansive vision of education, by enhancing—not diminishing—the authority and judgment of those who know our children best. We need to examine the varied meanings of trust and carefully rebuild, one by one, schools that are trustworthy. For children, there is no shortcut to becoming thoughtful, responsible, and intellectually accomplished adults. What it takes is keeping company with adults who exercise these qualities in the presence of adults-to-be. As Mike Rose notes in his indispensable book *Lives on the Boundary,* "To have a prayer of success, we'll need many conceptual blessings," above all a "revised store of images . . . that celebrate the plural, messy human reality" of educational excellence. I hope to give the reader, from my experience in schools, images of trustful multiage settings very different from those we now hold in our heads.

The message of this book, then, is not "just trust us." The title, with its echoes of "in God we trust," is a provocation, not an invocation. Our schools must never be beyond question, argument, debate. First, our schools don't deserve such trust; second, I don't think it would be healthy for us to invest such trust in any secular institution, and surely not in any democratic institution. I invoke the religious parallel as a challenge: What kind of trust can and should we have in our schools? What kind of trust should we practice within their walls? The trust I have in mind is not based on blind faith. It is a hard-won, democratic trust in each other, tempered by healthy, active skepticism and a demand that trust be continually earned—what school people these days call the demand for accountability. Trust is thus a goal and a tool. If there is faith involved in the kind of trust I have in mind, it is faith in the extraordinary drive and capacity of all children to learn and in the ability of ordinary adults to be powerful, active citizens in a democracy. This trust demands that we cope even when trust is occasionally betrayed, as it inevitably will be, if we want schools that enable kids to cope with modern and democratic life, and if we want this for not some but all kids. The schools whose stories this book tells are all public schools built around trusted adults. They are merely a small sample of the thousands of such schools in this nation, whose stories we too often ignore. These are communities that are warily, often quarrelsomely determined to stick with each other for the sake of the kids. Within these communities, teachers are encouraged to talk to each other, debate things of importance, and use their judgment on a daily basis. Parents meet with teachers frequently and press for their own viewpoint. Sometimes they make trouble. Kids learn the art of democratic conversation—and the art of passing judgment—by watching and talking to teachers whom the larger community shows respect for and who in turn show respect for their communities. Principals are partners with their faculties and have the respect of their communities. Everywhere you look, in such schools, people are keeping company across lines of age and expertise. Innumerable casual as well as formal interactions take place between generations. And there are plenty of checks and balances to support appropriately skeptical families, citizens, and taxpayers. But the bottom line is, the school has sufficient authority to act on its collective knowledge of its children.

Of course, all this would be irrelevant if this kind of trust did not help schools teach what children need to know. But it does. The kind of trust I explore in this book, in all its varied shades and meanings, has enormous educative value. Children in the schools I have worked in, and in many others like them, thrive as learners—many more children do, in fact, than ever did in traditionally organized public schools.

I know that even the best of these adults in the best of these schools often feel on the defensive, half ready to give up acting like grown-ups and just do as they are told, pull back into their shells, or quit. And that is not merely a result of the society's attitudes toward schools. The reality of life in many of our school communities—mirroring, as they do, the life of the larger society—is that it's difficult, fraught with the potential for disappointment, conflict, and frustration. Organizing schools around collective decision making among teachers, having teachers be responsible for each other's work, inviting parents into the life of the school, balancing the authority of professional and lay leadership, dealing with often sharp differences—all these are enormous challenges that never go away. What staves off discouragement, when so often working against the grain, is the pleasure we get from the company we keep—colleagues, kids, families. It's hard to hang out with kids all day without wanting to surround them with a loving and beloved community.

That's the topic of this book: the complicated nature of trust as it pertains to schooling. This topic requires exploring the varied meanings of the word itself and reminding ourselves of its proper contradictions and limitations. There are appropriate and inappropriate levels and forms of trust for any situation.

It's not that I take to trust naturally or easily; neither do I find myself comfortable appealing to it. Quite the contrary. I knew from the day I began my encounters with public education that there had to be a way to make schools "trustworthy enough" for me to remain both a public school parent and a public school teacher. I also knew that trust couldn't mean abandoning my skeptical mind-set. If I trust myself, which is the most important starting place, it might require being distrustful on many occasions. When a mechanic I barely know is annoyed at me because I don't trust his judgment, I sympathize with him, but I get a second opinion anyway. When friends worry over whether they can trust a politician on the basis of how that politician comes across on television, I remember my mother's words—"they've a track record, that's where you look to see if you trust them." If this made good sense a half century ago, it's far more pertinent in today's world of virtual realities.

I hope to show in Part One what schools built on the premise of trust—with all its warts—might be like and why trust is intimately connected to cognition—both social learning and academic learning, as well as the fundamental and daily challenges involved in building trusting and trustworthy communities.

In Part Two of this book, I hope to demonstrate that the alternative —trust through testing—can't work. The misplaced worship of the

quasi science of testing, I will argue, threatens to undermine the very
accountability it was designed to serve and to increase, not decrease,
the growing quality-of-life gaps that bedevil so many of our children
in school and outside of school. Standardized testing and the systems
built around it are the latest obstacles facing us, and they threaten to
engulf the energies of teachers in a fruitless and counterproductive attempt to beat the test rather than take on the unfulfilled task of educating all children well.

Finally, I tackle the ornery public policy implications for "scaling
up" the kind of work that rests on fallible human judgment—and
the messy in-betweens required to make schools trustworthy enough.
This book is also an urgent plea for seeking solutions compatible with
the survival and nourishment—some might even argue restoration—
of democratic public life.

I'm unabashedly hoping to convince you that it's possible to raise
our kids another way. The way I suggest would even be cost-effective,
and the necessary trade-offs would be quite tolerable. That this approach happens to be good for most kids, while critical for the most
vulnerable, also makes it a good political sell. Such small and rooted
school communities are not escapes from the larger world but the best
possible training for coping successfully with such a world. And when
we succeed in building such communities, not only do our children
become more skillful but also we have helped them imagine what a
world writ large that shared such trustful values could be like.

PART ONE

Trust and the Culture of Schools

CHAPTER ONE

Learning in the Company of Adults

One afternoon I find myself approaching a group of young teenagers hanging out in our hallways. They aren't hanging out surreptitiously. They are not always within earshot, but they frequently make it known that they are nearby, where we adults are also hanging out—fixing our rooms, meeting together informally, arguing about some important matter or other. They give me the distinct impression that they want both to have their own world and to be sure it is connected to ours.

Still I am obliged to remind them (and myself), "School was over an hour ago. You can't hang out in the school like this; it's not safe." I mean safe for me, of course. I am worried about liability issues. Some years earlier an amused but genuinely curious adolescent boy had even put the irony into words for me: "Do you mean it would be safer for us to be out on the street?" So as usual I let it go with a warning that neither they nor I take seriously.

Two things move me about the memory of these events, and countless others like them: the genuine, heartfelt desire of young people to be in the company of adults who are doing adult work, and the way our institutions and adult lives are structured more and more to keep us at a distance. As I think back on more than thirty years in schools, I believe that the contradiction between these two facts is the central educational dilemma of our times. In those boys' desire to hang out with and around adults lies the secret, the key to transforming our schools—and the key to the best avenues to learning.

A television interviewer talking to a group of high school dropouts some years ago asked them whether they knew any grown-ups who were college graduates. They all said no. Not true, I thought—since, after all, they had known a dozen or more teachers over the years, all of whom had attended college. But I was wrong. As I began to pay closer attention I realized that of course they had not *known* any of their teachers. We adults were invisible to them. In commenting to a friend about how disrespected I felt when some teenagers poured in the subway car playing loud music, using what appeared to me inappropriate public language, and dressed to shock, I was reminded that, alas, my assumption that they were doing this "to annoy" might be wishful thinking—maybe they didn't really register our presence at all.

It's a striking fact that kids don't keep a lot of company these days with the kind of adults—in or out of school—whom they might grow up to be (or whom we might wish them to grow up to be); in fact, they don't keep genuine company with many adults at all beyond their immediate family. Our children don't work alongside adults in ways that, for good or bad, were once the norm for most young people in training to become adults. Even when they take jobs, it's usually in the company of teenagers—at a Gap or McDonald's.

Is this phenomenon truly new? Yes. And does it have an impact on the trust necessary for good schooling? Yes again.

A century ago, even less, children made the transition to adulthood early, steeped in the company of adults. Surely by fifteen or sixteen, when a majority of youngsters today are still a half dozen years or more away from entering the adult world, most were already in the thick of adult lives: having children, earning a living. They spent their time in the midst of multiage settings from birth on—small communities, farms, workplaces where they knew grown-ups intimately and knew a lot about how they went about their work, negotiating their way through life. Being young in the olden days wasn't idyllic, not by a long shot. It's useful to say this to oneself over and over. The early immersion in adulthood that characterized life a century ago was for many a source of enormous pain and hardship. Good people worked hard to help create a longer and more protected childhood. But for good or ill, until quite recently, most of the learning of how to be an adult took place formally or informally in the company of grown-ups—by working alongside them, picking up the language and customs of grown-upness through both instruction and immersion, much as they had learned to talk and walk.

Children once learned the arts and crafts of being a grown-up by belonging to a community whose habits and rituals they naturally absorbed. When I was born, the majority of young people even in the United States never attended high school, and what they learned from formal schooling was a very small part of what counted for getting on in the world. Usually the trades they went into were ones they were very familiar with and had observed for many years, and thus taking on adult burdens came about gradually, step by step. The passage from being a novice to becoming an expert was often very gradual and had little to do with formal schooling. Children gradually absorbed— sometimes uncomfortably—the skills, aptitudes, and attitudes that went along with membership in the "club" of adulthood, in psycholinguist Frank Smith's apt metaphor. They found the present and future predictable and, at least in that sense, trustworthy. However conservative a vision such a style of learning suggested—generation following generation in orderly progression—it was the way most humans learned for centuries.

In seeking a substitute for the natural learning communities of yesterday, we invented schools and then systematically began to downgrade anything learned in nonschool ways. Schools bore the burden of replacing many if not most of the functions of those former multiage communities—and at increasingly earlier ages. In a daunting but perhaps not surprising twist of fate, the schools that replaced those natural learning communities simultaneously underwent a transformation too—toward greater depersonalization.

Formal learning in particular deliberately ignored what might have been the strengths of the traditional routes from childhood to adulthood. Most children today are disconnected from any community of adults—including, absurdly, the adults they encounter in schools. Many young people literally finish four years of high school without knowing or being known by a single adult in the school building. Dry textbooks and standardized curricula unconnected with any passions or interests of children, delivered by adults in seven, eight, or sometimes nine 45-minute time slots, dominate schooling.

We've invented schools that present at best a caricature of what the kids need in order to grow up to be effective citizens, skillful team members, tenacious and ingenious thinkers, or truth seekers. They sit, largely passively, through one after another different subject matter in no special order of relevance, directed by people they can't imagine becoming, much less would like to become. The older they get, the less like "real life" their schooling experience is—and the more disconnected and fractionated. As my granddaughter Sarah tells me with delight at her new eight-period schedule (which she knows I disapprove of): "But Grandma, it's more fun; there's no time to get bored—you're in and out so fast, and you get a chance to chat with friends between classes." Children are expected to learn to do hard things in the absence of ever seeing experts at work doing such things—to become shoemakers when they've never seen shoes or a shoemaker making them.

We've cut kids adrift, without the support or nurturance of grown-ups, without the surrounding of a community in which they might feel it safe to try out various roles, listen into the world of adults whom they might someday want to join as full members. At earlier and earlier ages they must negotiate with a variety of barely familiar adults, increasingly barren classrooms, and increasingly complex institutional settings; for many it starts as early as three or four years of age. My grandson, in a big New York City elementary school, spent his seven-year-old energies finding ways to avoid the halls, bathrooms, lunchroom, and recess, where everyone he encountered was likely to be a stranger—and a risk to his sense of safety. In some communities kids go from one huge school to another every three years—by design. Large schools designed exclusively for kindergarten through second grade, grades three through five, grades six through eight, and grades ten through twelve are not weird aberrations but are increasingly common. There are nowadays fewer children in schools where there are likely to be teachers they or their families have known over the years. We are—in short—perhaps the only civilization in history that organizes its youth so that the nearer they get to being adults the less and less likely they are to know any adults.

I believe this needn't be; schools can turn around the distrustful distance that the young experience toward the adult world. They can return children to the company of adults in ways that meet the needs of a rapidly changing and more globalized world. It's not true that the best way to learn to deal with adult change and trauma is to know nothing but change and trauma. In fact, quite the opposite. Greater, not less, intimacy between generations is at the heart of all the best school reform efforts around today and is the surest path to restoring public trust in public education—while also enhancing the capacity for creativity and novelty, which earlier forms of apprenticeship learning often downgraded.

The kind of company I want children to keep with adults is essential to learning. And the key building block of this relationship between student and teacher is trust. The more complex the learning, the more children need genuine adult company, and the more trusted the adults must be.

Polly Wagner, our school's math consultant, noted that seventh grader Jerry was busily doing his geometry assignment but seemed to have no idea what an angle was. But what's so puzzling about an angle? So we explored it with Jerry. For one thing, it's the first time he's ever run into a measurement that stays the same even when what's being measured appears to get bigger. It took a while for his teacher, Emily Chang, to figure out how to explain this to herself, then to us, and along the way to a puzzled Jerry. As Emily pointed out, in some self-astonishment, it isn't a measurement "in that sense." Aha, I said. We tried to define different meanings of "measurement." There we were, three adults and one kid, puzzling over and complicating what had seemed to us so obvious until we looked at it through Jerry's eyes.

What is the setting that allowed Jerry to explore the obvious more fully with us, and to have his confusion taken so seriously? Furthermore, what was required for the adults as well to find each other's company so trustworthy that we stopped for a moment to consider our own confusion? What allowed us to reconnect to the sense of surprise and wonder that is at the heart of human learning?

The key was that we risked showing ourselves to be learners alongside the student. We teachers made it acceptable for Jerry to ask questions, because we so clearly were asking questions we didn't already know the answers to ourselves. There is no way to get around it: the willingness to take risks, ask questions, and make mistakes is a requirement for the development of expertise. We can learn secretly, but at a price. If we act as if we take it for granted that there's never (well rarely) a "dumb" question, just occasions when it is hard for us to understand where we're each coming from, then we can more readily go public with our confusions. And confusion is essential—if uncomfortable. It's the frequent outcome of allowing ourselves to pursue our curiosity more deeply, to pay attention to the unexpected. Whatever do I mean by "up" and "down"? Why is it that I can forever go east but not forever north? Am I wrong that the sun used to rise over that building and now it doesn't? However can it be that a big heavy metal boat doesn't sink?

Living without answers is unsettling, of course, but when we're not required to immediately pretend to master uncertainty, and probably only then, we can make the slow intellectual leaps required of all children today. It's not a luxury that only a favored few need, as it may once have been. The trustful relationship with the world that this acceptance of uncertainty allows—with respect to people, ideas, and things—is at the heart of learning.

Lots of successful students probably never really trusted teachers or school systems when they were kids; still they got by and even did well. How come? In part because kids were once school successes even if they never took more than a year or so of math beyond arithmetic, at most a year of science, and one or two courses in history. Most of what life required us to learn happened over time in authentic, natural settings. Furthermore, what the most successful students had going for them was that even in kindergarten, with their hands eagerly raised, they were ready to show off their school smarts. Starting on day one, certain forms of knowledge and skill—the stuff they've eagerly brought with them from home—was confirmed and honored, thus increasing their self-confidence to take still more risks. What they were good at grew out of trust—it's just that the trust came from something or someone outside of the schoolhouse.

But many other students never found a replacement for a school and teacher who didn't recognize their genius, who responded with a shrug or a look of incomprehension as they offered their equally eager home truths. They too soon learned that in school all they could show off was their ignorance. Better to be bad, or uninterested, or to just silently withdraw.

Today schools are expected to impart, even to five-year-olds, more complex, bookish, abstract knowledge than ever before, including much that is counterintuitive. Children in today's science-rich world even need literally to unlearn what some learning theorists call "cognitive illusions" common to our "native" minds—prescientific assumptions about how the universe works that are at odds with the realities of probability theory, modern physics, and biology, and a good deal more. As these demands on content increase, the gap between the well educated and the pseudoeducated threatens to widen even earlier. I want us to imagine what it would be like if we were to create environments that fostered learning because of—not in spite of—school, that took advantage of what we know about how all children best learn and what all children can contribute from day one, so that all children will maintain their trust in their own learning abilities and in the families who are their first teachers.

I enjoy telling all who will listen the startling fact that kids, rich and poor, learn new words at the amazing rate of about ten per day from the time they first start understanding speech until their early adolescence, when the pace slows down. It's so counterintuitive that it takes repeating often for the importance of this fact to sink in. I didn't accept it right away myself. So-called dumb kids do this, as well as smart ones, kids from disadvantaged homes and kids from wealthy homes (although which words they learn may differ). Now that's a feat no school or schoolteacher I've ever encountered has matched. And not only do they learn ten a day, but they don't forget them. (Linguists measure accumulated word recognition—tallied annually—and then divide by the number of days in the year.) At school we'd be thankful if they learned ten a week and still retained them a week later.

I'm told we can learn this astounding amount of vocabulary because our brains are wired that way. When people acknowledge this fact, they often suggest that it's somehow peculiar to learning our spoken native language. But I think quite the opposite. If kids are wired in such a way for the development of spoken language—and all the ideas, concepts, faces, names, and places implied in the process—we'd do well to pay attention to these natural ways when we organize learning in the formal setting of school, including for reading, math, and science!

The way children best learn the complex skills and dispositions of adulthood is through keeping real company with the kinds of experts they hope to become (and, incidentally, through keeping company with the real things of the world—the malleable and predictable—although occasionally surprising—stuff of which the world is made). The amazing thing is that we no longer trust these ways of learning.

Think how efficiently virtually all young people learn to drive a car if they have lived for years in a family of drivers, have ridden in the front seat, have imitated (both in their heads and in their bodies) the motions of a driver, have gotten a feel for where the sides of the car are and how close the outside world is. When my mother finally suggested I should move into the driver's seat, I, like so many of my friends, already knew how to drive—except I was surprised when I tried to restart the car on a hill (this was in the days before automatic transmissions), plus there were the mysteries of parallel parking. If we were to stop to think about all the discrete skills we internalized when we were pretending to drive, it's actually both staggering and scary. Some of us need not much more than a few hours of formal instruction! In contrast, people who come to driving without having had such exposure have a hard time learning and are often handicapped for years by not having this natural sense. Sufficient naive trust in the other drivers on the road is probably also essential to skillful driving and can come only from years of reinforcing traffic experience. It helps also if the driving teacher—formal or informal—is someone you respect, has little reason to believe you will probably fail, and will not benefit from your failure. And keep in mind that despite the cost we almost never try to teach anyone how to drive except one-on-one.

Lots of tasks that we think of as fairly simple seem so only because we learned them in settings like this. Cleaning house, folding fitted sheets properly, and even doing the dishes—not to mention cooking—are more complicated than we usually realize. Depending on the culture we grow up in, we naturally learn different but equally complex skills—many of which are unacknowledged by the larger world, if not literally devalued as trivial. Some kids use the same techniques they use at home for learning new things, even in quite traditional schools—learning on the sly through listening in when other kids are on the hot seat, copying from peers, waiting until after class to ask a trusted friend to explain—except we think of it as inappropriate to learn this way in school. In every class I've taught, a few kids (usually boys) creep up behind me to listen in while I am teaching another kid, muttering the right answer under their breath. When approached one-on-one, they clam up. If we begin to see all the kids who come to us in school as possessing quite remarkably complex skills that are springboards to doing equally well in a host of new learning topics, we'd be on our way to imagining new ways to approach teaching.

Why we join some clubs and not others is an intriguing question. Probably it depends a lot on how long we stick around, which in turn depends on how unconditionally we are welcomed and how much we are trusted to have what it takes. Do the more expert members see us as one of them? Are they flattered by our efforts to copy them, or do they shoo us away or scorn us for our stumbling tries? Above all, do they take it for granted that we'll get the knack of it over time? The more these qualities are part of the setting, the more efficiently we learn.

Learning happens fastest when the novices trust the setting so much that they aren't afraid to take risks, make mistakes, or do something dumb. Learning works best, in fact, when the very idea that it's risky hasn't even occurred to kids. After all, babies learning language or learning to walk don't consciously muster up courage to take risks —they are simply safe enough to do what comes naturally. They count on us to keep danger at bay. Our parents are delighted with our silly mistakes—our malapropisms. They assume that most of what we can't do is not out of orneriness, lack of natural talent, or bad intentions, but that we are not yet skilled enough. We will get there. No one is sorting or ranking us, and we are not confronted with much that is out of our family's control, stuff that is arbitrary and could hurt us. We're in the company of the people who are most firmly on our side, no matter what.

There is no way to avoid doing something dumb when you are inexperienced or lacking in knowledge, except by not trying at all, insisting you don't care or aren't interested, thinking the task itself is dumb (not you), or trying secretly so no one can catch your mistakes—or offer you useful feedback. Of course, these are the excuses we drive most kids into when they don't trust us enough to make mistakes in our presence. Clearly this is also a list of ways to reduce the opportunity of becoming more skillful to nearly zero—except for some extraordinary autodidacts who can make their mistakes in the privacy of their own minds. Isaac Newton at seventeen learned most of his early mathematics and physics through reading page by page from Descartes's geometry—out of the sight of Cambridge's esteemed math teachers, who deemed him mathematically weak. Only then did he venture forth among his peers.

Even learning the role that making mistakes plays in learning is best learned by observing experts making mistakes. But we usually make such critical knowledge invisible. To prove that light is essential to life, teachers the world over place some plants on the windowsill and a control group in the dark. But alas, when I tried this, the ones in the window dried up and the ones in the closet flourished. I secretly tossed them away overnight so I could redo it to turn out "right." My favorite college physics teacher did the same thing when his demonstration lesson on falling objects didn't work. He tried a few adjustments and then ruefully promised to "show it to you again next week." What he and I had in common was an unwillingness to do that "figuring out" with our students, which would have been the really important experience. We both believed, perhaps, that our students wouldn't trust us if we exposed our fallibility, or perhaps we overestimated the danger of students seeing the wrong answer. We acknowledged the importance of trust, but we thought it required that our students see us as infallible. It's not just that kids have a hard time believing that their teachers use the bathroom, but that their teachers learn the same way they do, and that it's what we do with our mistakes that makes us worthy of our authority.

All of these details requires a community of presumed equals—equals not in knowledge or expertise but in that deeper sense that anyone of us could find ourselves in the shoes of another, that we are members of a common community. Kids need to hear adults say—and mean—"what an interesting way to think about this" rather than "you couldn't have been listening if you think that." Taking interest in wrong answers increases the odds that we will have students' energy on our side, which in turn allows us to feel confident that most children will fill in for some of our mistakes and lapses as teachers—which under the best of circumstances are many. We have to trust students' drive to learn, because it is the greater part of what we have going for us.

If what I've been saying is true, then dramatic changes are required in schooling—both in curriculum and in pedagogy, what and how—above all in the relationships of learners to teachers, teachers to families, and teachers to each other. There are schools that have made such dramatic changes in their own often quite different ways—all radically different from what we now see as "real" school. (Kids sometimes tell me that our school is not a "real" one. It amazes me to see even four- and five-year-olds play "school" with a scolding teacher barking orders to their untrusting charges.) Despite vast differences, there are some commonalities in terms of the relationships between teachers and learners in the schools that work to build the intellectual skills of all kids.

First: schools that work are safe. We know that infants require safety to thrive, but so do school-age kids. The more time that must be devoted to protecting oneself from bodily or mental harm—from peers or authorities—the less energy there is left to devote to other tasks. Creating safety for kids with a diversity of histories and goals means more than just making them physically safe—it includes helping them to feel safe from ridicule and embarrassment.

Second: schools that work do their best to reproduce the ratios that make for successful learning—that is, the number of experts per novice. That means not only the ratio of teachers to students but also the range of expertise available to kids—other adults, older students, and students with different skills and abilities, not to mention varied learning tools (computers, books, real-life learning experiences). The ways are varied: small classes, multiple-age classes, older students working with younger ones, adult volunteers, activities that cut across age and skill levels. Successful schools are always looking for those magical relationships—the ones that break down the barriers.

Third: schools that work make it possible for those precious experts—even if they are only slightly more expert—to show their stuff, to display and demonstrate both their passion and their skill in highly personal ways (not just to talk about what they're good at but actually to do their stuff alongside of novices). Sharing expertise—copying— is viewed not as cheating but as a useful way of learning. We learn best alongside people we rather like, who can't resist showing us this or that amazing pattern even, if it isn't part of their official duty. Coming across hundreds of snails in our schoolyard for the first time launched an unexpected but irresistible study of snail life. How wonderful it was for our children to learn that there are famous scientists who study snails (and make a living at it) all their lives.

Fourth: schools that work offer a range of ways for learners to find their way around any new domain of knowledge, and more than one way to become good at science or history. Successful schools take it for granted that mistakes have a logic to them that needs to be uncovered, not just corrected. Placing objects such as a nail or a heavy box or a sliver of wood in a body of water and exploring what happens, probing tactfully—"what would happen if you added this?"—can lead to fascinating discoveries, but this approach takes expertise, plus an open scientific mind-set, if it is to lead to "aha's" for most of us. Even then not all of us will come to the aha's through one particular experiment alone. There need to be other openings for discussing the differences between density, mass, and weight—which initially may seem identical. When a thirteen-year-old said to me over lunch the other day, "Do you know, if I tried to count to a billion it would take me a lifetime?" how delighted she was that after all these years of being an adult I was for a moment skeptically astonished. But she's right—as we figured out together. Whether we take in new ideas as babies by exploring the nature of the objects in our environment with hands and mouth, or later on by measuring objects on a scale, over and over again, or by calculating how many seconds it would take to get to a billion, we are doing the same thing: making ideas ours. Once they are ours, they don't seem counterintuitive anymore—or, equally important, they don't seem like nonsense. We now have a basis for making sense of not just this one thing but many more.

Fifth: such schools offer plenty of time for ideas to grow, and they don't set rigid timetables. For some kids the aha's are almost immediate; others require seemingly endless repetitions—just in case next time it will come out differently. Besides, such qualities of patience are to be cherished and are, after all, part of the scientific tradition. Although making a flat map out of a round globe does what no book-based explanation of map distortion can achieve—try it!—it's a waste of precious time if we think about it as an exercise in coverage rather than in understanding.

Sixth: schools built around this model of learning do their best to make schooling engaging and fun. Engagement and pleasure help focus the mind, keep one persevering, and encourage repeated practice.

Pain may occasionally teach us a lesson, but not as a regular routine, and the lesson it most often teaches is avoidance. This means filling up the classroom with stuff of interest that couldn't help but fascinate and leads to questions, ideas, experiments. It means including both ordinary materials—sand, dirt, and water—in new contexts, more exotic ones—centipedes and monarch butterflies—that amaze, or unusual ideas that can't actually be seen or touched but fascinate—like the distance to the moon. And adding to these collections of things and ideas are all those books—including beautiful ones—that might illuminate students' questions. It helps (for many reasons) for kids to see themselves, their communities, and their stories reflected in what is studied—but often in new and unexpected contexts. Ulysses' boasts are familiar, after all, as he endangers himself and his men just to get in the last word to the Cyclops. Good schools have ways to latch on to kids' idiosyncratic passions as well—their love of cars or wrestlers even—in the formal instructional day as well as after school, on Saturdays, and during the summer.

Seventh: such schools know that what one is learning needs to have lots of possible hooks to other things and thus lends itself to being practiced in the normal course of living. Suddenly, as soon as you're studying a new subject, it seems that the whole world is talking about what you've just learned! Studying about American politics when it's election year or the Supreme Court when there's a major debate over who is to be selected to sit on the high court make getting the most out of such subjects far easier. My high school teaching colleagues and I missed a great opportunity in the early nineties when we ignored the breakup of the Soviet empire and just kept on with our self-prescribed course of study. We did better when the world became so much more frightening for us all on September 11, 2001. We took the time to explore the unsettling immediacies of the moment in depth and thoughtfulness with our older students. (For many teachers of tenth graders these days, changing the course outline in light of the changed course of history is literally to risk children's educational futures—and their own—in light of state exams.) But studying about ancient Greece last year for all the kids from kindergarten through eighth grade didn't seem irrelevant either. The students ran across so much stuff with Greek motifs in the daily press, magazines, buildings, stories, and everyday language. I have seen elementary school students and high school kids take to ancient Egypt with an even greater zeal. It turns out to be a favorite regardless of age, second only to dinosaurs—so there must be hooks we don't always recognize.

Those seven, plus that love which doesn't allow us to give up, is all there is to it, except that it's very hard to see how we can organize schools around these ideas. In fact we have organized our schools around precisely the opposite ideas: passive learning of curricula designed to cover an unrealistic amount of material, therefore discouraging exploration and understanding. That's the startling and disturbing fact. And the poorer the kid, the more likely she is to be a person of color, the more disadvantages she otherwise has in life and the more likely the school is to ignore all seven of the above ideas. Not to mention the pernicious influence of standardized testing and its associated regimes, which systematically work against environments built on trust—supposedly, but as we shall see, falsely, in the very name of trust—once again, above all for those students most in need of and dependent on good schooling.

But since the schools we have today are a relatively new invention, and in fact the ways I'm proposing come from an older tradition, I believe we can reinvent schools to better conform to what we know about teaching and learning. Such reinvention will require patience—because it cannot be imposed on unwilling subjects, be carried out by teachers who are opposed to it, or by communities who see it as a threat to their children. And this reinvention will be hard even for the converted to do when in part they still are beholden—as we all are, consciously or unconsciously—to quite different theories of teaching and learning ourselves. Whenever I say "One teaches best by listening and learns best by telling," I startle myself and others. I know I'm right, but it's very hard for me to practice what I preach. At the moment it goes against so many of the conscious tactics used for formal learning that I experienced in school.

Hardest of all, the task of reinvention requires the creation of an adult culture that matches the one we are trying to organize for the children. It requires, to be truly efficient, that a child's in-school and out-of-school worlds overlap and sometimes even merge. It takes putting kids and adults into a shared community in which they are all members, albeit with different levels of responsibility and skill, different kinds of authority, with each accountable for different parts of the whole. And it takes trusting in our children's vast intellectual potential along with our innately human drive to understand and master.

I've seen it happen. It can be done.

CHAPTER TWO

Experiments in Trust:
The Mission Hill School
and Others

A ll over the nation there are those exceptions—places that have held onto sane-sized, humanly scaled schools. Some are great schools. A few are probably awful. Others are merely good schools—meaning one would be willing to have one's own children spend their time in them. Many are rural—the places that resisted the consolidations that swept the nation after World War II and picked up steam in the sixties and seventies. Some, of course, are private schools, independent or religiously based.

The small schools I know best, however, are public schools, intentionally invented after bigness was the norm—starting in the late sixties and early seventies in cities and suburbs all across the nation. They were created from scratch in part because smallness was appealing, but mostly because they represented a different vision of what it meant to educate all children well, and what it would take to do so within the public sector. And at the center were a series of ideas about the educative importance of respect for the human penchant for learning and about the role of adults—at home and at school—in preserving and extending this natural talent.

Of course, there have always been kids who make it despite what appear to be adverse environments: big impersonal schools or schools that perhaps purposely insist that children renounce their home culture. There are kids who even seem to benefit from keeping school and family in separate airtight compartments. But for the vast majority of learners, it helps when their learning works in concert with their home and community, not in conflict with them, and expands upon the learners' known universe, rather than denying or trying to forget a part of it. And for this to happen, adults in schools need to truly know the children they serve over many years, something almost impossible in traditional huge schools.

My experience with putting these ideas into practice beyond my own classroom began with efforts to create small adult communities within big anonymous city schools. Creating interesting places for teachers to learn was where my reform agenda began. An extraordinary woman named Lillian Weber was teaching early childhood education at City College when I arrived in New York City in the fall of 1966. She pointed to the loneliness of the teaching profession as a serious roadblock to good work with children. It isn't enough, she insisted, that we love our own twenty-five to thirty children, or even that we respect their families, although those were necessary starting points. Weber argued that both children and adults needed to be part of a community of learning. Her wedge into the big schools was called the "open corridor." She found principals willing to put three, four, or five interested teachers, often of different grade levels, next to each other along one corridor—and then added student teachers from City College. She ensconced herself in the corridor and began to demonstrate, play, talk, discuss—while ostensibly supervising her student teachers. She created communities of adults and kids where their respective work was public and visible to families, colleagues, and peers. She built minischools in these corridors. They were fragile, rarely lasting more than a few years, but they whetted our appetite for more.

Lillian made us pay attention to all the learning that was taking place quite efficiently in unexpected places, the instructive interactions that we didn't count as instructional time. We were reminded of the extensive evidence of the centrality of play in human learning— and the terrible cost, both emotional and intellectual, when playfulness is aborted too early and too often. She made us more aware of what kids already knew before they arrived at school and what they continued to learn before and after school from their families and communities. We began to think in new ways about our own learning histories, our enthusiasms and confusions, and how we could learn from other adults in ways that could make the school a productive complement to children's learning.

Central Park East (CPE) grew out of Lillian Weber's work; this school was simply an "open corridor" that was more permanent, less dependent on the annual vagaries of a principal. District 4 in East Harlem, considered at the time the least successful district in New York City, made me a proposal: would I like to start "my own public school"? It was too appealing to turn down—especially given the gathering storm clouds of centralization, back to basics, and more and more testing that was driving the system in the early seventies. I gathered friends from Lillian's workshop center at City College. We asked only for rooms near each other, enough autonomy to work out another way of teaching kids that might get better results, and a system whereby parents would be given a choice about joining or not joining our community.

In less than five years there were three elementary CPEs in East Harlem, and shortly afterward we organized a CPE secondary school (CPESS), and over the next few decades dozens and dozens more on the same model just in New York City. For a time, our bottom-up reform ideas were even faddishly popular, as the various standardized solutions bottomed out. It became commonplace to hear college education majors talk about starting their own little public school, as though this were one of the long-standing career options available in life. (And, we would argue, had the policy arm of the educational establishment listened to us and devoted anywhere near the same energy, focus, and resources as they periodically devote to standardization, the total number of such little schools would have increased exponentially.)

What these schools set out to do, although they weren't always aware of it, was to tackle the problem described in chapter 1: to change the nature of the company kids and teachers keep, to build a trusting and trustworthy community, and thus to help children learn in more efficient and natural ways. In the year 2000 the nearly forty small New York public high schools that came out of this period of work put together sufficiently compelling data to convince even a group of reputable and established test experts gathered together by a hostile commissioner of education that they were onto something important. The schools' graduation and subsequent college attendance rates, for kids that met everyone's definition of "at risk," were hard to explain in conventional terms. Of Central Park East high school students, for instance, 90 percent graduated and 90 percent of those went on to college, in a city where the average dropout rate was 50 percent. The group of test experts convened by the commissioner to put an end to these maverick schools came out in tentative support of them instead. What they were witnesses to, I claim, is the power of such schools to build relationships that educate, in contrast to institutions that can't because they are organized to ignore, if not exclude, such relationships.

In 1994 I retired from teaching in the New York public school system to join Ted Sizer at the newly funded Annenberg Institute for School Reform in order to support efforts to make such forms of schooling more systemically feasible. But one day in the spring of 1996 I found myself on a long drive to Boston—with a broken radio. So I had time to dream, and I found myself dreaming of starting another elementary school. By the time I got to Boston, I was bursting with the idea. Boston, I knew, had just begun a little systemic approach to reinventing schools, sponsoring small pilot schools with much of the autonomy of charter schools but embedded firmly within the city's public system. It was the brainchild of the local Boston teachers' union, and it was hard to resist. At sixty-five, I found the idea of taking on a new little city appealing, and Boston wasn't much farther from my new home base in upstate New York than New York City had been. I gathered some Boston and Cambridge friends, we wrote a proposal, and we were accepted—to start a pilot school in the fall of 1997 in an old vacated church school in the Roxbury section of Boston. The building would be shared with a new pilot high school. Between us we'd have about 350 students, a floor each to ourselves and some shared spaces. I was back to where I began, with a few differences, principally a much more conscious awareness of the issues of account-ability and trust. When I started at CPE, I had mostly been focused on simply creating a safe haven for me and some friends to do what we thought right. The student population was somewhat different too—although overwhelmingly a population of color, there were fewer Lati-nos, more middle-class students, and more whites—20 to 25 percent.

The Mission Hill school, like many of the other small schools I know, was deliberately designed to make it hard for the adult culture and the youth culture to hang apart for long. We even tried to make it easy for the high school and elementary school to exchange people and ideas. We shared a secretary the first year, and a social worker, a nurse, and, above all, ideas and camaraderie. Even in terms of physical space, we thought about how to make the generations overlap. At Mission Hill Elementary, the main office—located right in the heart of our main floor—serves as the workspace for the full-time administration (me, Brian Straughter, and the school manager, Marla Gaines), as well as a portal for parents coming and going, for teachers picking up mail and using the copier, for most phone calls, not to mention being the place "bad" kids cool off, good kids retreat to, and everyone leaves mes-sages—who's out that day, who has gone to do an errand, and so forth. The grown-up behind-the-scenes life of the school is made visible and touchable. Kids come in and out to use the copier, the phones, and just to say hello and see what's up. We don't have to lecture them about this place belonging to all of us—it does.

We got this idea of shared space in part from Urban Academy, a small high school in New York City, where the staff have desks sur-rounded by their own bookcases and file drawers, a niche that ex-presses their unique interests, all in one huge room. The kids come in and out to see teachers and discuss their work. It's like the floor of the stock exchange. Everything that's going on is right there. Usually hushed and quiet and busy and important. The Mission Hill main office is a miniversion of that.

The hallways and lobbies of such schools work best if we think of them as the marketplaces in small communities—where gossip is exchanged, work displayed, birthdays taken note of; where clusters of kids and adults gather to talk, read, and exchange ideas. It's Lillian Weber's "open corridor" forty years later. Mission Hill's hallways are a marketplace of goods and ideas that cross ages—from the youngest to the oldest. We were lucky because the seventy-five-year-old building was designed with fourteen-foot-wide corridors.

We organized our very small school into two even smaller identical clusters, each occupying half the floor. Half the five-year-olds start with Alicia Carroll, with whom they spend two years; then they move across the hall to Emily Gasoi (and now Jenerra Williams) for two years, then on to Alphonse Litz, and finally to Ayla Gavins and Heidi Lyne and the middle school team. Four or five teachers thus get to know eighty kids so well that being accountable for them happens naturally, without complex articulation plans or reporting schemes. In schools in which children work with new teachers every year, each teacher would effectively have to get to know twice as many students. In addition, the Mission Hill teachers know exactly where the kids they have had for two years are headed next—right across the hall. At the other end, Kathy Clunis, Geralyn McLaughlin, James McGovern (and now Matthew Knoester), Roberta Logan, and Emily Chang constitute a second minicommunity. The seventh and eighth graders naturally grow into being the leaders of the school—taking on new jobs as they seem appealing and useful. A group of kids begged (Tom Sawyer fashion) to organize the end-of-the-day bus dismissal—which involves having to use cell phones. Others took on our Friday morning assembly, where students share work in progress—leading the littler kids in singing songs the older students might shun if they were only part of the audience.

We aim to create an intense adult community of learners that will entice kids to want to belong too. To increase the odds, we are constantly on the lookout for ways kids can join adult activities wherever we can find a space or interest. When we're all studying about ancient Egypt, the hall turns into the Nile River with important landmarks along the way, and amateur Egyptologists join us. Joyce Stevens, our curriculum consultant, is often ensconced in the hall, a la Lillian Weber, with odd and interesting objects and an inquiring mind.

It grows. Youngsters at Mission Hill borrow the computers in the class next door or the office when their own are being used. They stop to chat with grown-ups, take books from the library, read what is on the walls—kid stuff or grown-up stuff—take pride in knowing everyone and being known. Because all of us, from five-year-olds to seventy-year-olds, study the same Big Themes at the same time, the corridor takes on a unifying role. The big schoolwide themes are both enticing and constraining. We ask ourselves often, is the trade-off going to be worth the loss of the individual teachers' autonomy to decide what to concentrate on? Are schoolwide themes developmentally sensible? Just as we ask ourselves whether the easy access kids have to the copier, the phone, and our semiprivate messages might sometimes backfire. Some of these practices, after all, were dictated more by lack of space than by design. But as time passes, we see these by-products as plusses (although with occasional misuses!). As you walk down the halls of our school or schools like ours, or in and out of these classrooms, you are struck by how much conversation is taking place and how often it crosses age boundaries. Kids begin to use grown-up phrases, to try out the intellectual jargon of their teachers—at least some of the time. Of course, one reciprocal effect is that we adults also find ourselves slipping into the jargon of our youngsters.

It mattered that as a Boston pilot school we were allowed to pick our staff, develop alternate school-based policies where our working rules conflicted with the teachers' union contract, use our equal per capita funds more flexibly, and in general more or less set our own course, within the confines of Massachusetts state education law. We receive no more money per student than any other Boston public school, but we made spending choices that allowed us to reduce class sizes by effectively hiring more teachers. Doing so meant that from the start we reduced class sizes to twenty students (compared with a citywide average of over twenty-five) and added a full-time paid adult-in-training to each class. Some of these adults came from regular teacher education institutions, and some came just to explore the possibility of becoming teachers. We also discovered that class sizes and pupil-teacher ratios are like closet space—critical, and there's never enough. We didn't have to scramble for a building, although of course we had to hustle to see that it was properly remodeled, renovated, and kept up. That first fall we opened without furniture.

Maybe even that scarcity helped in the end more than it hurt. You can see the effects by looking into the classrooms—even today—with their eclectic mixture of tables and chair styles. That first September teachers hurriedly built colorful benches—with the kids (it's now become an annual practice). They put cheerful curtains and plants in the huge rotting window frames. Unlike traditional classrooms with rows of chairs and a desk at the front, the spaces that emerged from the beginning easily accommodated each teacher's style, as well as a variety of teaching and learning styles for kids. Meanwhile parents went looking for books with which to fill our beautiful mahogany-shelved library—scrounging from neighbors, famous people, and local libraries in lieu of city funding for libraries. (The city was far more generous with computers—which arrived even before we made a request.)

The touches of beauty in this old former Catholic high school inspired us all—the woodwork in the library, the hanging lamp globes in the corridors (that gave, alas, insufficient light), and the stained glass windows connecting two rooms on the top floor, to mention just a few. While the building is basically a very ordinary-looking, even shabby stone rectangle, these spots of elegance add some intangible pride to our concern for our school.

Much of the day kids are working independently or in small groups, which probably is one reason visitors think we have few serious discipline problems or especially needy or learning-disabled youngsters. Both are harder to detect, although in fact our student population is pretty representative of Boston's overall demographics. (Our students are chosen through Boston's universal citywide lottery system based, in part, on parental choice, and over which we have no control.)

Given the importance of adult talk time, we put aside monies that in another school might have gone into hiring another staff position in order that each full-time core faculty member was paid to "think like a principal"—for the time and extra work involved in intimately being a part of and responsible for the conduct of the whole school—from designing curriculum to evaluating colleagues. The freedom to allocate our funds in our own way made it easier to ensure that we'd put in the extra time that any good school needs from its members. Researchers have noted that American schools expect teachers to spend more time instructionally and less time preparing for their work than any system in the advanced world. We decided to do something about this. The Mission Hill staff agreed, regardless of stipend, to work together for five hours a week after the school day was over, as well as three weeks over the summer, one professional retreat day midyear, and the regular citywide professional days. It turned out to be not enough. But it meant we could move into ways of working that many of the teachers had never tried before, to create a community for adults and kids alike around common topics, to be largely self-governing—and thus accountable far faster than otherwise. If trust requires accountability, accountability requires time.

Of course, spending more on staff development and planning time—and smaller class sizes—meant spending less elsewhere: we hired no full-time specialists in foreign languages or physical education, and we had no self-contained special education services or supply clerks. Even music was reduced to part-timers. We bought fewer individual student and teacher desks, and we spent virtually zero on individual class textbooks.

The extra time together as teachers meant we could immediately tackle the question of the standards for graduating our eighth graders. We designed a system, modeled roughly on the one we used in New York City's small high schools. We started with many fewer older students, so that we could try out our graduation requirements first on a small scale. In June 2001, all twelve of our first graduates completed the arduous, pioneering adventure (some of them complained of being "guinea pigs") of preparing, presenting, defending, and in many cases re-presenting many times their six portfolios before their Graduation Committees. These six portfolios are aimed at demonstrating to a committee of five (composed of one external critic, a younger student, two faculty members, and a family member) that the student has lived up to the school's standards of work and habits of mind in history, literature, art, science, math—plus something we've called "beyond the classroom." In each area, graduating students need a body of work that demonstrates consistent habits of work and intellectual competence, as well as the ability to present and expand on such work in a public way. The record of this committee's findings and the student's work become part of the school's permanent archive. We also videotape a sample of sessions for our own and public purposes. We held our breath near the end. The first twelve, just barely making their deadlines in time to cross the stage at our first graduation, moved on to a high school of their choice.

We also undertook to develop varied ways to collect hard data. We interview—on an ongoing tape—every child as a reader twice a year. We collect and score writing samples. We conduct standardized math interviews. We hold exhibitions of children's work. We visit each other's classrooms. We invent questionnaires and surveys to tap into student engagement and family connectedness. We compare our hard data to the test data we also have and any other available standard indicators—attendance, transfers, tardiness, suspensions. We do this mostly to improve our work, and to see whether we have confounded the odds that predict that some kids won't reach high standards. We look at the data in every which way—separating them by class, race, gender, and how long kids have been with us. This wide range of evidence of student work is our way to demonstrate to children's families and the broader public our trustworthiness. Its value lies precisely in the fact that it is open to different interpretations and judgments.

The judgments we make are exercises in the use of the same five habits of mind we commend so highly to our students: (1) looking at the data from several different viewpoints, (2) questioning the validity and reliability of the evidence, (3) looking for patterns across subjects and time, (4) making hypotheses, wondering how else we might have done something, and how else it might have turned out. In the end the work must meet the test that "it matters." This fifth habit of mind is perhaps the one that's hardest for schools to get right, and the most important to the kids.

Thomas Friedman writes in a recent *New York Times* essay about a teacher of literature and journalism who changed his life, and whose classroom was the clubhouse for her devoted fans. She was old, crabby, tough, and decidedly unhip—but she offered something that shaped these budding intellectuals and journalists. Of course, many of those who passed through her classrooms never caught what so drew Friedman. Her mind and heart couldn't have reached out year after year to a new 150 each term.

In a small school like Mission Hill, kids can pick and choose, as over the years they develop new relationships with the adults—some like the tough lady of Thomas Friedman's memory, and others prefer the young and hip. In a school purposely designed for falling in love with new experiences and people, the odds of each student finding a life-changing adult outside of his or her family circle is extraordinarily great. When students are preparing to graduate, we select an adult who is not currently one of their teachers to act as adviser, to guide them through the portfolio process. We also picked up on a successful CPESS practice—community service. Invented as much to provide teachers with free time as anything, it turned out to have life-changing repercussions for entirely different reasons. Over the four years that students spent doing community service, almost all, according to in-terviews conducted in later years, had built at least one relationship with an adult that helped them get into college, find a job, build a network in the larger world. We fashioned something similar for all youngsters in grades six through eight at Mission Hill. In addition, our part-time school social worker, Delores Costello, uses her knowl-edge of kids and families to find all manner of experiences for each family and child—scholarships for one-of-a-kind sleep-aways (e.g., Alvin Ailey camp), Saturday art programs, or museum offerings. We brought musicians into school so that kids could sit at their feet, listen, watch, and imagine being them (which led, in turn, to hiring a string teacher to teach violin and cello). As the graduates of Central Park East reported to us years later in trying to account for their unusual success, the school had not only acknowledged and nourished their own particular interests, but also sought ways to link them to other people who in the end were life-inspiring.

Boston's Isabella Stewart Gardner Museum, with its stuffy nineteenth-century unchanged European art exhibit, has become a familiar second home to many of our students, thanks to the imaginative adults who have organized its education program. Our kids go there now, greet the guards and curators with respectful familiarity, and make themselves at home in the best sense. Parents tell us that when they go to the neighboring Museum of Fine Arts kids casually guide them through the familiar Egyptian exhibit, the ancient Chinese rooms, and the Greek sections—comparing, contrasting, and pointing to particular beloved works of art they have become familiar with. Students tell stories, based on close observations over the years, about our neighborhood and Boston, stories connected to schoolwide themes about the history of Boston and its people. All of these cultural experiences are powerful because they are mediated by relationships with people the students have come to know and see as familiar.

When we first began to work in Bronx high schools ten years ago, creating small high schools out of the large, anonymous James Monroe High School, we were shocked at how our students viewed Manhattan—as an alien and distant world that didn't belong to them, although it was only a few subway stops away. They lived within very circumscribed boundaries within the world's most cosmopolitan city. We found links to Manhattan for them, visiting museums, parks, architectural sites, special neighborhoods, and stores. All these experiences help kids to own a larger portion of the world, to imagine themselves at home in places that once seemed hostile or just foreign. These are experiences that cannot happen successfully without the mediation of trusted adults—family and school. Adventures into "other" worlds can be destructive as well as instructive without the right company.

A staff that looks and sounds like the kids and their families, in terms of race, style, and ethnicity, is another asset when trying to build trust. At Mission Hill the majority of classroom teachers and administrators, for example, are people of color. This is the fastest and most efficient way to assure kids that the experiences the school opens up for them are not always "white" or "black," but belong to them all. Having a staff that even partially mirrors the makeup of the students also increases the odds that the conversations among the adults partake of the languages the children are accustomed to at home and see as theirs. I realize how nice it is that talk in the high school lapses into Spanish so often. Using the students' own languages sends reassuring messages. It allows some things to go unsaid while sending a message of respect.

A group of school people from Oakland, California, who are seeking to turn all of Oakland's schools into small, mutually respectful learning communities, visited us recently. What one of them said struck me deeply: "We need," she said, "to hear about what goes wrong, problems you maybe didn't solve, the mistakes you made, and that's what we appreciate most from our visits to Boston's new pilot schools." So, with that in mind, here are some thoughts on mistakes and problems. Of course, the mistakes are usually one-of-a-kind. But in the early years of a school, there are bound to be many, and they are likely to be more serious than similar mishaps after a school has taken fuller shape and has a track record to fall back on.

You can't do everything at once. Getting our professional act together in the early years of both Central Park East and Mission Hill meant that we didn't give some parents the kind of insider feeling they needed from us. Achieving a good balance between staff governance and delegating responsibility takes time, and is dealt with only if you make the time. But making the effort saves time and trouble later. Even the way we sold the school to parents led us to hyperbole that I'd avoid next time. We appeared to be promising what could only be long-range hopes. "But you said kids would stay with a teacher for two years," some parents noted when a teacher left after their first year in the class. It helps to be cautious—to spell out more of the downsides. How to be both supportive of one's colleagues and also accountable for their work—to be friends but also critics—has to be confronted directly, and often. Good and well-meaning people don't do it naturally. Talking about race and racism up front won't settle things, but edging away from it until we trusted each other better was a mistake. The absence of more than token bilingual staff also hurts. Finally, it's never too soon (or too late) to tackle the question of how leadership is passed on, what happens when the founding principal leaves? Each of these issues consumes time.

Our mistakes were compounded by the fact that we opened Mission Hill just as the impact of so-called standards-based reforms hit —with the advent of the Massachusetts Comprehensive Assessment System (MCAS), a grade-three-through-twelve testing program with high stakes attached. It was a testing system antithetical to everything Mission Hill represented in terms of both curriculum and pedagogy. The new and controversial regime required working out a stance that could be supported by staff and parents alike. Although many opposed the tests, some parents also feared for their children's futures in a society that would judge them by their test results. Such concerns had to be taken seriously. Faculty members also worried about making kids take a test that they had intentionally not taught to the way other colleagues in the city had—especially in history and science. The debate was time-consuming but necessary. Our school was clearly running against the grain of a testing system built on distrust, and it not only made us bristle but also conflicted with our methods and aims. Our site-based board came up with a partial solution: the school was directed not to test any child whose family asked to be exempted. After coming out near the top among local city schools in reading and math in the year 2000, in the fourth year of the test, 85 percent of the families sent a letter saying "no, don't." (It may be that our relative success—no one in the state did very well—made it easier for families to join a protest movement.)

It turns out that while the state mandates that schools give the tests, it doesn't mandate penalties for the kids who don't take them or their families. At worst, our practice lowers our cumulative school score (since students who do not take the test are given a zero score), and thus our ranking, and could perhaps (if the city or state chose) lead to threats against us. If we were a high school, of course, the risks for kids and families would be greater. Many families choose for their kids to take one or another of the other standardized tests periodically administered in Boston just to see how they stack up, and we regularly provide families and kids access to tests if they want to see what they're like. On the whole we were able to provide some evidence for our claim that kids would do as well in the long run even on tests. It remained hard for parents, kids, and teachers to operate against the grain, but doing so enabled us to avoid having to reorganize our curriculum or pedagogy to match the frequently changing state frameworks and tests. (In some states, penalty-free opt-outs for parents are now state-mandated.)

The ancient Greeks knew what they were about when they said that democratic governance was the province of the leisured classes. (The word for school and leisure are one and the same in Greek.) It takes time to be thoughtful. How can space for the exercise of judgment in governance be translated into school life? This is our number one problem. It will be yours too, we told the folks from Oakland. We wanted a leisurely lunch and recess time for the kids, but we wanted the same for the adults who worked in the building—time to go to the bathroom, to use the phone, to get hold of needed supplies, to talk to colleagues, or just to eat in private and sublime silence. We managed it. But we still ache for more adult leisure time to work things out, and finding ways to staff the kid part of that midday break is full of trade-offs. Of course, we'll never know what the other side of all these trade-offs might have produced. So we try to forgive ourselves for our failures, even as we keep them in view.

Different schools will invent different ways to establish their unique culture—often diametrically opposite ways—as well as make their unique mistakes. That's a hopeful fact rather than a discouraging one. The kids find calling us by our first names an important symbol of our shared culture, for example. But I know that the kind of learning environment we have created here also exists in schools that insist on last names, even uniforms. What doesn't work are schools that think we can be made uniform, that the messy business of learning to deal with each other can be bypassed by rules imposed by people who don't know us in all our particularities.

In a school with so much easy access to each other, the odds are that it won't always be smooth going—maybe sometimes even less so than in big and more impersonal schools. The culture of a school that is organized the way Mission Hill is brings questions of trust—between parents and schools, among teachers, between children and teachers—to the fore in a way that is perhaps unique in American education. The power of trust makes these schools run and makes them educative. The potential pitfalls that come with trust are what make them difficult—and exciting—places to work. As the following chapters explore, the way trust plays itself out, or not, is all in the details—and the details, almost without exception, are never finished.

CHAPTER THREE

Parents and Schools

L ike the adage "all children can learn," "parent involvement" is a sacrosanct part of contemporary educational rhetoric. Both phrases have the blessings of educators, citizens, and politicians of all political persuasions including some of my favorite researchers, school leaders, relatives, and friends. I quibble over the fact that the first is an incomplete idea, with little meaning until we know what all children can learn. But calling for more parent involvement is also an incomplete idea until we ask similar questions. The Mission Hill School is founded on a vision of community that includes parents. But includes them in what, how, when? Should parents have a say in how I do my job? In what ways? These issues, as much as any, go to the heart of trust and schooling.

So where do I stand? Uncomfortably.

Certainly I know that my stance depends a lot on which side of the fence I'm thinking from: as a parent and grandparent or as a teacher and principal. As a parent I felt sure I knew my kids as learners better than their schools and teachers did. The problem probably got worse because we changed cities and schools so often in those early years. So when my son's third grade teacher claimed he needed remedial reading, I knew she was not merely wrong but bizarrely so. He was a fluent bookworm, read practically anything he could lay his hands on, and clearly understood it in the way that any eight-year-old might if it was read aloud to him. The last thing he needed was remediation, especially in a school system where many of his classmates were barely reaching independence as readers, much less fluency, or love of books. But the experience reestablished for me my confident view that one doesn't simply leave such matters in the hands of professionals. (For this bad attitude, I later learned, my son's permanent official record card had me down as a "troublemaker.")

During the same period my father underwent a serious operation at a highly reputable New York City hospital. Just before the operation, I visited him and felt deep concern—something seemed seriously wrong with his state of mind. I was assured that it was not atypical before an operation and might be the result of a mild sedative he had taken. Since he never came out of that fog after the operation, it seemed probable that what he had experienced was a slight stroke before the operation and a major stroke during it. I learned a lesson about "who knows best." This, as well as a series of other experiences, helped me decide a few years later to take my sonogram to a few consulting doctors before I agreed to an operation for ovarian cancer. Five doctors read the same test results and came to three different conclusions—not about what they saw but about the treatment plan to follow. I followed the one that seemed right to me—or maybe just what I wanted to hear.

In some ways these experiences confirmed my support for parental choice in education—for shopping around, getting second opinions, and above all being allowed to select a school that matched a parents' biases and inclinations. I saw no contradiction between this and support for public education. Public schools simply had to be redesigned to offer families more choices, just as medicine should. Even if the number of choices were limited, and no parent could be guaranteed to get exactly the school he or she had in mind, why not do the best we could, I thought. I still think so.

But choice doesn't necessarily imply a specific role for parents once a school is chosen. That's where things get subtle and messy. I was able to choose between doctors, but no doctor thought that once I had chosen him or her that I should be calling the shots. Some barely thought I should be consulted. At some point I had to relax and trust to the judgment of the physician I had selected. Of course, recognizing this fact doesn't turn me into an easy patient, a fact that makes me sympathetic to difficult parents.

At Mission Hill we insist that parents visit before they make any final decision, although the citywide mandatory choice system does not require this. Why? So they can look at our classrooms and ask, am I comfortable leaving my kid in this place? It's a question not of agreeing with everything we do, I tell them, but of feeling safe with our making important decisions. I tell the story of me and my mother, whose child-rearing approaches I was determined in many respects not to follow, but whom I felt comfortable leaving my children with for long periods of time. I told my own kids, with confidence, "In Grandma's house you do things Grandma's way—even if it's not my way." In fact, there were limits to even that familial trust; my mother and I certainly fought over issues from food to discipline. And I am not my students' grandmother. I view the question "Am I comfortable leaving my child here?" as at best a starting point for negotiation and an entry point into the question of trust in the professional work of teachers.

What I offer as a teacher, after all, is not just an acceptable baby-sitting experience but rather, like my doctor, professional expertise. What kind of evidence of my trustworthiness can parents legitimately demand? What kinds of questions are they entitled to have answers to? How should parents balance trust and skepticism? How should teachers balance autonomy and professional pride with responsiveness? What kind of relationship between parents and teachers is best for children—no matter how difficult it may be for either of the adult parties involved?

First, it must be made clear that openness to a family's questions and concerns—even about what makes us trustworthy—is a constituent part of being a good teacher at any school, not just an attractive add-on. It's part of the business we're in.

If the capacity of doctors to listen to my story, to ask good questions, to assume that I am a good informant about my own health, and to put up with my need for information and even second opinions is actually relevant to their providing the best care, then the same is even more so for teachers. In the end, I decided, these traits—the so-called human relations aspects of doctoring—were part of what make some people better medical diagnosticians and better-informed practitioners, not just more comfortable ones. Their skills in this area were intimately related to their being able to apply their expertise. By now I have a whole host of anecdotes to back up this viewpoint. So I feel more, not less confident that being a "difficult" patient is not such a bad thing.

The same holds true for teaching and schooling: listening to families is more than a favor to parents; it is essential to children thriving as learners. Listening to the family is the only way to get the full picture of the child, an understanding of how what we do at school might fit or not fit into what is likely to happen at home. Since children are educated four-fifths of their waking lives outside of school, families are, in the end, primarily responsible for the education of their children. When school people ignore this, they are undercutting the effectiveness of both school and home.

But even after we get through the school and family introductions and establish the principle of collaboration, it isn't smooth sailing. The family is still endlessly negotiating how to translate the differences between school and home in a context fraught with judgments of the highest order—is this teacher or school good enough, competent enough, well intentioned enough, or smart enough to count on? For elementary school teachers, there are twenty to thirty different such families every year who are passing judgment on them—and whose support the teachers' success depends on. (The numbers are far higher in high schools, but teachers are probably less aware of such judgments since they see so many students—well over a hundred—each semester.) And to make matters worse, even in those cases where choice is open, it's not so easy to just drive out and try another school or teacher, as you might with an auto mechanic. Teacher and family are pretty much stuck with each other—at least for the year.

Furthermore, teaching and parenting are highly personal callings. Teaching is not merely a job. Teachers are giving not only their knowledge and know-how but their affections and respect. Their weaknesses and shortcomings are easily exposed. They sometimes overlook or ignore an individual child's needs in favor of the group's needs—or even the needs of the school as a whole based on their assessment of the situation. They are calling upon one set of prior experiences rather than another based on often insufficient evidence. Act they must, every second they are in the presence of the children—for better or worse. And how they act in that classroom is the sum total of who they are. Parents are unavoidably judging the whole person, not just the service delivered.

But the reverse is also true. Teachers are passing similarly sensitive judgments about the families they serve, with at least as critical a nature, and with potentially devastating consequences. Two groups, usually of women, are thus thrown into a relationship in which both feel at times inadequately prepared and vulnerable to each other's discerning eye.

It's no wonder that for many teachers, parents are a source of acute distress and discomfort. Even if 90 percent of students' families love you, the fact that the other 10 percent do not is not just a passing inconvenience but an endless wound that never quite heals, and that still aches sometimes even years afterward. For some parents, anxiety about school haunts them, in turn, as they try to imagine a way of intervening on their child's behalf without counterproductively annoying school or teacher.

It's tempting under these circumstances to create institutional distance—in myriad big and small ways. And it's important to acknowledge that schools that effectively create such barriers—through sheer size, as well as through other formalities that make contact difficult—can often paper over such dissatisfactions more easily and on the surface run more smoothly, saving themselves and families a lot of hurt personal feelings. This effect may partially explain why school systems and parents like to think that, at least by the time children reach high school, parents are superfluous—kids need their independent space (even though the evidence suggests that teens may now need families more than ever—if differently). Many of those who argue for maintaining big impersonal schools are quite conscious of the advantages that accrue from precisely these barriers to our knowing each other better. I have recently reconsidered the fact that I have no formal office. My easy accessibility sometimes feels like a handicap, if I'm honest, because it removes the formality and spatial intimidation that a desk in a big office offers.

This mutual personal vulnerability is only one part of the equation. Relationships between families and schools mirror all the other divisive categories and vulnerabilities of the society writ large. The African American families I first worked with on Chicago's South Side soon told me how little their own parents had trusted the schools they had sent their children to. If they acted "as if" the school was always right and their kids always wrong, it was not a sign of trust. They did not take it for granted, as my family did, that the teachers and schools were allies, doing their best (even if it was sometimes inadequate). Some suggested that it had been better in their grandparents' day, in the old segregated South, where the schools may have been unequal in every way but the teachers esteemed members of their own community.

For many of the families I first encountered as a kindergarten teacher at Chicago's Beulah Shoesmith School, the school was alternately ally and enemy, and it wasn't easy to know which. Parents couldn't assume that the people in the school viewed their child as an attractive, lovable, and intelligent being. An African American neighbor and friend of mine reminded me, when I asked why she dressed her daughter up so elegantly for school, that the teachers at our shared, largely low-income African American school wouldn't mistake my daughter's casual dress for lack of care or sufficient money to dress her well, but they might make that mistake with her daughter. She had a point.

The history of helplessness in relationship to officialdom was only just beginning to be challenged on a wide scale by African American parents when I began teaching in the midsixties. The message to "do as you're told; don't get in trouble" had a double edge. "Because I won't be able to back you up even if you are right" was the unsaid second half of the admonition. That, African American colleagues told me, was what lay behind what so annoyed me—their apparent docility in the face of school authority figures and the compliant behavior they demanded from their children. My naïveté in failing to see the price that they and their children might have to face if they engaged in the kind of responses I thought natural and appropriate took me time to understand. Like all rage long suppressed, it soon reached the boiling point and exploded—a mere few years later—in the bitter racially charged school wars that pitted black parents and community activists against schoolteachers and school boards in so many of our cities in the late sixties.

For most of my teaching and parenting life I've worked and lived in communities in which I was in a racial minority. While the majority of the students at the schools I've worked at and that my children attended were African American, with substantial Latino minorities in some cases, there was no way that I could thoroughly appreciate the ways that race impinged on our interactions. For Latino families, racism and cultural differences, as well as prejudices based on linguistic ignorance and biases, add to the equation—not to mention the impact of not being able to communicate in a shared language. Even when my white colleagues saw themselves as actively opposing racism, the subtler forms of racism and class bias, not to mention distance in lifestyles and experiences, made it quite possible for us to misunderstand and be misunderstood, despite our good intentions. Surely parents were often asking, what assumptions about their lives and viewpoints was I making, and how did these affect my teaching?

The history of racism in general, and the daily examples of racism I witnessed in the schools I subbed in for two years before I became a kindergarten teacher in Chicago, were ample enough reminders that the fears of African American and Latino parents were not paranoia— had such reminders been necessary. I could guess from my own war stories as a parent that my experiences could be amplified many times over and still only scratch the surface of some of the fears parents must have been repressing as they enrolled their children in Central Park East or Mission Hill. Nor was it possible for me to know when the rifts between us were because of race or class, just natural suspicions toward those who play such potentially powerful roles in our children's lives, or the result of my individual faults.

In my first year of teaching I met a mother and child at our local supermarket shortly after school was out for the summer. We chatted amiably, and then she asked, in a halting and embarrassed voice, why it was that I had taken a dime from her daughter early in the school year and had never given it back. I was taken aback. In fact, it was quite possible that I had done this. I have since frequently reconstructed the possibilities—of taking away the dime because she was playing with it inappropriately, with the promise to return it when she went home, and then, at the end of the day, in the frantic stress of getting all thirty-three children ready and out the door on time, either forgetting or even ignoring her request for it! What was interesting to me was that it had mattered—to both mother and child—but also that she had waited to ask me until her child was safely out of my classroom.

In fact, I run into difficulty with families whose race, class, and ethnicity match my own and whose distrust is perhaps of a quite different order. Maybe the very sense of entitlement that whiteness and class give them make them less concerned about trusting my intentions—which they take for granted—and more concerned about my competence. Or maybe they just want to be sure we leave no stone unturned, no opportunity missed that might advance their child's interests. Especially in this anxious and individualistic period in our history it's hard for these parents to view the school as a community that must serve all children and not to zero in first and foremost on where their child ranks in comparison to other achievers. The impact of this all-too-human trait is that some parents, with more time, expertise, and a sense of entitlement, will garner disproportionate resources for their kids. For example, Mission Hill, like other schools in Massachusetts (and perhaps the nation) confronts the reality that a surprising amount of its state-mandated special education funds now go to children of middle-class families and white children whose families have learned to turn what was once thought of as a stigma into an advantage. The privileges that power carries with it are hard to unravel. As an actively involved parent myself, I realized how much more likely my children were to get special treatment in such matters, for example, as teacher assignments. We were simply more in the know. Parental "involvement," in so many ways critical to good education, can, in other words, potentially increase existing inequities.

Is it that less privileged families would not dare to be so demanding, or does their less privileged position in the power structure suggest a different lens for viewing life—a more communal one, characterized more by social solidarity than by individualistic advancement? Is that a romantic interpretation? It is also possible that African American and low-income families took less seriously our promise of a rose garden, our description of the ideal community we hoped to invent, and had fewer options to compare us with. But the open-ended distrust that middle-class white families often express and the distrust that less-entitled low-income minority families feel for all institutions make for difficult school and family interactions—and thus for learning problems.

As with my doctor, the issue isn't only personal trust—knowing that my doctor cares about me and is there for me at all times; it's also a question of trusting her competence. Kids go through school only once, and every night parents wonder—did I do right? Even if this teacher likes my kid, does he know how to teach him to read? For some this includes wondering, should I have made the sacrifice and paid for a private school? Schools of choice compound the potential for guilt: did I make the right choice?

The best of teachers have, on occasion, lost a child on a trip, been partially at fault for a child's missing his bus at 3 P.M., yelled at a child when he or she actually wasn't wrong (and could after all have been spoken to in a calmer voice). I'm reminded of my own parenting failures. I remember the time it was my turn to pick up the kids at nursery school and discovered, after dropping them all one by one, that I had

forgotten my own. When I returned to pick him up, I saw the knowing look and raised eyebrows that passed between his two teachers
("Ah, these busy parents"). Maybe it's because mothers know their
own failings that they are nervous about those of surely less loving
professionals.

On both the social and academic fronts I have certainly failed families. We had a student for several years who was teased mercilessly by
his peers. I finally urged the family to transfer him, because I could not
find a way to stop it and believed he was coping with it in a way that
was bad for him and his peers. Having subsequently read more about
this phenomenon, I now think I could have found a better solution.
Similarly, I knew from the first moment that six-year-old Robert was
going to be the prototypical bad boy if we didn't act fast to shore up his
academic skills. I took on the task of tutoring him, and yet it was two
years before I accepted the fact that my expertise was not up to pro-
ducing a breakthrough in literacy, by which time damage was done
that more expertise might have avoided. We learn from these experiences, but our learning curve may not meet the needs of the particular
families involved or their children. This hindsight wisdom is hard on
teachers and parents; it undercuts our stance of professional expertise.

Causes for concern are endless. Every time we—the staff at Mission Hill—come up with a great solution to a problem, we know we
need to anticipate an angry response from some families. We groan,
"Oh, those parents." Some, we suspect, just feel left out—ignored and
disrespected because we spent so much time talking among ourselves
before sharing our thoughts with parents. But sometimes, of course,
the solution is good for the school as a whole, but it is not necessarily
the ideal solution for each and every child or classroom. We forget that
it's tough, and maybe unnatural, for parents to think first in terms of
how the school's health as a whole benefits their child.

We recently proposed job-sharing as a solution for two teachers
who each needed less than full-time teaching schedules. We thought
we had an ideal twosome—a pair whom parents knew and trusted.
Weren't we putting the interests of teachers above those of children?
some asked. The "we" versus "they" was—to us, surprisingly—quick

to surface. Some never gave up the feeling that they had been cheated of one person's full-time devotion. (One parent said that a teacher with an outside avocation—in this case it was music—shouldn't be teaching.) On the other hand, parents' objections forced us to be clearer and more explicit about why we thought the idea was good.

Similarly, a decision, in the interest of reducing class size, to move some children from one House (cluster of classes) to another met with a cry of betrayal that surprised us. By stressing the value of two-year continuity and the close-knit House structure, we had in some ways created an unanticipated problem for ourselves. Maybe we had to re-think the solution by adding other resources to the overcrowded class-room rather than making changes to balance the numbers. More docile parents would have been nice, but maybe we wouldn't have learned from the experience, and some children would have felt exiled and would have suffered for it. Involving parents in interviewing new teachers makes the process more complicated, sometimes unnecessar-ily adversarial, formal, and time-consuming, but it also usually wid-ens the focus of the inquiry in useful ways. I could go on and on.

I have some ideas about what it will take to make the relationship between teachers and parents work, if not more easily at least more productively. Here are some suggestions for schools and parents nego-tiating trust in close quarters.

First, schools need to be clear about their agenda—how they de-fine what they mean by being well educated, how learning best takes place, and what they think learning looks like at age five, ten, or eigh-teen. We're so used to considering schools only by comparing test scores or college admissions or the selectivity of the school's admis-sion practices that most schools—public or private—either forget to say what their goals are or fail to take the needed time to get it said so they are understood. But since parents may get the educational philos-ophy they sign up for, they need to know what the school's long-term goals are, what a successful student knows and can do. We try—each year more clearly—to put this into explicit parent-friendly language, without oversimplifying or watering down our ideas. We keep longi-

tudinal folders of student work and successful graduate-level portfolios. We videotape some of the graduation committee proceedings so
we can share both the process and the quality of work involved with
other parents and external reviewers. We know that not all will agree
with our judgments or with the conclusions of each committee. Judgments are by nature fallible. What parents will be able to decide is
whether the ranges of wisdom and error seem acceptable—and match
their broad definition of the purposes of education. This could be part
of what all public schools are required to present to families.

Second, we all need to be clear how decisions are made, even if all
schools shouldn't have to decide things the same way. Of course, clarity doesn't solve everything. Parents who know that certain decisions
are made by the staff still feel wounded and left out if their input has
been heard but ignored. And staff feel irritated when the same complaints (suggestions?) are made year after year. Also, as one parent recently told me, "I was hoping it would be more like home-schooling,
with the school being the site for me to school my children alongside
of the professional staff." We were a disappointment, although in ret-
rospect this parent was more sad than angry. We had, he admitted,
been up front about what he could expect, but he hadn't heard what
he didn't want to hear. We had one family who was convinced their
child was not learning to read properly, whereas the teacher thought
he was doing not merely okay but very well. We brought in another literacy expert whose judgment we respect, and she and I separately as-
sessed the child on a variety of instruments and materials. We couldn't
find a problem. We met on three different occasions with the family to
review the matter and ended up agreeing to disagree. We agreed not to
interfere with the form of tutoring they were going to embark on (a
highly structured phonics program we thought possibly harmful) and
to do our best to make the child comfortable during our language arts
time. We didn't relinquish our right to make such in-house decisions,
and we felt somewhat disrespected, but we also found a solution we
could all live with. (My very trusted family doctor made a similar deal
with me when I decided on acupuncture.) Probably many of us—
patients and parents—just go ahead, secretly using the acupunctur-

ist and teaching our kids the multiplication tables before the teacher thinks the kids are ready for them.

Third, parents must be given enough opportunities to feel comfortable that the school's and teacher's intentions are good, that staff members rather like their kids and expect a lot of them. As a parent, I know I read more between the lines than any reporting system was intended to convey about how well my child was just plain liked. I needed to know, were the teacher's values and mine in synch? All the various formats we use for reporting—regular lengthy family conferences, narrative letters, and more typical checklists provide information in ways that we hope help parents to know whether the child they know and the child we know are the same, or enough alike to feel we're on the right track. We read each other's reports before we send them out, to catch some of our own unintended and revealing biases—or just possible misunderstandings. Sometimes what we've said surprises us. But it's the face-to-face encounters that are the most critical—and hardest to rehearse—as are the opportunities to talk things over when misunderstandings occur, like why didn't you return a child's ten cents. Alicia starts each day with a quiet reading time so parents have something to do that's helpful when delivering their youngster. The regular family nights we hold at Mission Hill, when parents see other parents, teachers, and other children in a largely social setting, over food, help everyone to get a feel for who is who.

Being allowed to drop in occasionally can be reassuring for parents. It also helps to have children stay with the same teacher for at least two years—whether through looping, where a teacher moves up with a class; multiage classes, where children remain in the same class as seven- and eight-year-olds; small class and school size; or block scheduling in middle schools and high schools, where students stay with the same teacher for both science and math, for instance. All these devices increase the odds in favor of getting to know each other. Some of this is harder to accomplish for older students, but knowing your children are known well and liked is critical at all ages.

Fourth, all parents need ways to make informed judgments about the professional competence of the school. My decision to trust one of those five doctors' opinions as to whether to operate immediately was based only in part on the fact that I liked the advice (don't operate) and felt comfortable with the doctor. It was also based on what I knew about each doctor's reputation among other professionals, as well as how convincing I found the evidence each presented—or in some cases never even bothered to present. An incompetent doctor or teacher who likes you, and whom you like, is not enough. One reason not to leave your children even with a beloved grandma might be that as much as she loves them she's not up to it. The process of formulating judgments about school and teacher competence occurs on many different levels. Some of it happens informally—word of mouth, what neighbors and graduates say, as well as what parents notice regularly—what's posted on the school walls, what happens at school assemblies, and so on. Certainly as young people get older, their own competence as judges of their learning becomes critical feedback regarding the school's competence. At Mission Hill we provide families with access to the various ways we rate children's progress, as well as with our interpretations. We tape students reading aloud twice a year and translate the results into a report—a graph—showing student progress from kindergarten through eighth grade. We keep samples of student writing with our agreed-upon scores and examples of math work to back up our six-stage math assessments. The most powerful evidence of progress parents are given comes at the end of a student's career with us, when they sit in as members of our performance review, alongside teachers and outside reviewers.

Trust also relies on other evidence that the school knows what it's doing, evidence that is less centered on the performance of individual students and that provides ways for families and the public to judge a school's track record. Private schools—and many elite suburban schools—depend a lot on their reputation for getting kids into the right secondary school or college. But the typical public school has to be more convincing—and here is where a wide range of data counts, and many more kinds of data than standardized test scores. At Central Park East we kept long-term data on what happened to the kids who graduated from our school—at the end of sixth grade and twelfth grade—and received funding to publish the results alongside some fascinating interviews conducted many years after kids and families had left us. The stories of the remarkable real-world successes of those young people constituted the most powerful—if expensive—form of evidence we could offer.

Periodic professional school quality reviews—conducted by outsiders who come in for a few days to systematically make a report on the school—help in this regard. The credentials of the staff (like the licenses and diplomas on your doctor's office walls) probably don't carry a lot more weight than they do with patients assessing their doctors, but maybe they should. There's a public school in Manhattan —the Manhattan New School—that takes pride in publishing their staff's external accomplishments—papers written, degrees awarded, speeches delivered.

Fifth, parent-school relationships require lots of time. Lack of time can be a potent enemy of good school and family relations. Every demand for more attention from one family is time taken away from teachers who feel they are always juggling impossible demands. When my daughter went from teaching three-fifths time to teaching full time she called to tell me that full-time teaching was, by definition, an impossible job—it couldn't be done. Something had to give. She's right. I once calculated, for example, that to provide even humdrum homework every night requires several hours a day (to prepare, collect, review, and respond to it). Thirty kids times five minutes per child equals 150 minutes—two and a half hours. And for the same reason, the extra time spent to meet one individual child's needs is at the expense of another—another child at school or one's own at home. No wonder, then, that a parent with even an innocent question is sometimes treated like a nuisance. Sometimes finding time is so pressing that teachers avoid an issue—a controversial curriculum decision, book, or idea—because they know it risks time-consuming and important negotiations and explanations. Is it worth it, they ask?

Finally, there needs to be clarity about what to do when the quiet negotiating and compromising breaks down, and the school makes decisions that feel unacceptable or wrong. To whom might parents go for a second opinion? Whom does one officially appeal to for what? One answer at Mission Hill includes a sixteen-person board of governors—composed of five parents, five staff members, five community members, and one student. Parents can also always appeal to the superintendent's office. We've even had an occasional call from the mayor's office in response to an irate parental complaint—when a teacher or I handled something with undisguised irritation or in too much of a hurry. And there needs to be acknowledgment that there can be a time when an individual parent decides the school just isn't for his or her child.

It has taken years for the schools I know best to work through these issues, one by one, and then, since families and staff change, to revisit them over and over again. Such conflicts require defusing and reframing power relationships, finding time when there isn't any, and putting together structures that support each of these goals. And all of it must be done in a way that doesn't destroy the morale of edgy teachers, needy kids, and sometimes desperate families.

When the system is working, it makes the impossible possible. It was family support that allowed me once to pull four basically good twelve-year-old girls out of class for nearly a month to resolve an intolerable situation—to everyone's long-term benefit. The girls had formed a tight clique that was quietly threatening their peers and successfully and subtly undermining the class. The clique's leader was engaged in a battle of power with her teacher, who felt shaky about who was winning. With their parents' support, we spent a month demanding tough work from them, and we won them over—one by one—until they were ready to return to class. The girls were dubious at first about our ability to pull this off. But they were also relieved by the collaboration between school and family, which allowed them to revert to being—most of the time—smart and happy adolescents. Every teacher knows how much this matters.

Of course, what I'm passing over are the myriad ways in which schools and families daily resolve most of their issues because their kids are good go-betweens, all seems to be going well, and people hit it off. Perhaps the explanation rests, as much as anything else, with parents who know that if trust were to disappear they could not bear to send their children off to school every day, and what would they do then? It's partially blind faith, because what are the alternatives?

To be a responsible parent is to live with anxiety—anxiety that one's trust may be misplaced. For a school to make this less intolerable is far more difficult than the sloganeers suggest, and yet when we do it right, it pays off in remarkable ways. The answer does not primarily lie in more oversight bodies, on-site councils, and cogovernance structures. Schemes for increasing parental representation on governing boards have merit but have little to do with how all the other individual parents interact with their children's teachers or the school itself.

Getting the relationship with families right allows schools to provide the kind of education that can be transformative, that can truly make that other slogan, the one about how all children can learn, realistic without watering down our learning goals to trivial matters.

All this is part of a larger vision: that children can see the school as just one part of the larger adult company that surrounds and protects them, and thus as a place where they dare to challenge themselves to go beyond their customary limits, and even beyond the viewpoint of their families and communities—to explore the wider world. That's what schools are all about—and it cannot happen for most kids without their parents' permission, and it cannot happen well in schools that don't know and respect the strengths, knowledge, and skills that families offer their children.

The fences that divide us as parents and teachers won't ever be entirely removed—the central lens from which we view our schools will properly differ depending on our roles—but they can be far more permeable for the sake of our children's learning if we can get a better handle on trusting each other.

CHAPTER FOUR

Teachers Trusting Teachers

> Their qualities compelled by heart-conversation and laughter and mutual deferrings, shared reading, facetiousness alternating with things serious, heated arguing (as if with oneself), to spice our general agreement with dissent, teaching and being taught by turns . . . separate sparks into a single glow.
> —Saint Augustine, on his first intellectual community, from *Confessions*

Schools and school districts are accustomed to one-day retreats in which adults engage in exercises to build trust. I remember one in East Harlem where all the principals in the district were asked to get into small groups and share one secret they had never told anyone before. I walked out. As I told the deputy superintendent—who also walked out—if I hadn't told my secret before, this was surely the last place I would do it. I've also had questions about more fun exercises —like rope climbing or being led around blindfolded—as a way of building trust.

My distaste for many of these team-building exercises typical of professional retreats is partly just personal. But my objections are also based on my conviction that these exercises do not go far toward building the kind of trustworthy community needed to get the tasks of schooling—versus rope climbing—done. And finding a setting one feels comfortable working in, or even people you enjoy, may or may not be the goal we should be seeking, although it's hard to deny it as a value in itself. In other words, it's not self-evident that trusting someone at the other end of a rope translates into trusting one's colleagues in ways that lead to school growth. The kind of trust needed to provide important critical feedback, to share secrets about your teaching dilemmas, or to accept responsibility for your colleague's work may or may not lead to wanting to go camping together or confide a child-hood misdeed or a deep and powerful personal fear.

Just as we want kids to keep company with adults because it's the best and even most efficient way for them to become educated, so too do teachers need to keep company with each other for the sake of their teaching, not just to make life smoother, more comforting, and more humanly decent, although these other outcomes are desirable.

For schools like Mission Hill, in which the staff are required to as-sume substantial professional authority over each other and over the direction of the school, creating appropriate forms of collegial trust is a matter of the school's life—and death. But the kind of trust that fos-ters productive collegiality is critical not just to schools like ours, but to any school that wants to learn from its own practices, and for teach-ers who are seeking greater individual or collective authority to make important decisions about their work. In a paper on impediments to school change, Charles Payne and Mariame Kaba write,

> In one of its most instructive studies, the Consortium on Chicago School Research surveyed staff at 210 schools in an attempt to identify those charac-teristics shared by schools that were getting better. When the 30 most highly-rated schools were compared with the 30 poorest, a battery of questions about the quality of relationships proved to be one of the best predictors. While teachers almost unanimously agreed that relationships with their colleagues were cordial, that did not always mean they respected or trusted one an-other. . . . [Quoting the study,] "Teachers in the top 30 schools generally sense a great deal of respect from other teachers. . . . In contrast, in the bottom 30 schools, teachers explicitly state that they do not trust each other."

While Payne and Kaba remind us that these fractured relationships in schools are the outcome of many diverse factors, the results in terms of teaching and learning are striking.

We feel intellectual discomfort when our ideas are challenged—individually and collectively—in ways that can't easily be pigeonholed or dismissed. We can't fall back on "what science says," much less the principal. But this discomfort, what Cornel West calls the feeling of being "unhoused," pushes us to rethink old ideas, to go beyond clichés and preset limits on what's thinkable. It's the same kind of unsettling that Piaget argued was the driving force behind the intellectual growth of children—as they sought equilibrium when confronted by the unexpected.

The stories I tell come from the specific contexts of Mission Hill and other schools I have been part of, but I believe they have wide implications. Two intimately connected issues emerge when we think about the nature of teacher collegiality: the ability to critique each other's work as well as the ability to disagree about matters of importance to teaching and learning.

Friends versus Colleagues

At a retreat last spring, a principal of a small local Boston pilot school said aloud what others, indicating by their nods, were thinking. He commented that one trouble with small schools is that the tight bonds of friendship that they encourage among colleagues can also be dangerous to building good practice: friends might find it harder to hold each other accountable and to make tough professional decisions.

In fact, there are teachers I've known well who would have trusted each other literally with their lives but who didn't (and wouldn't) give each other useful feedback on their classrooms—or their views of each other's child-rearing skills. Interpersonal strife and hostility are surely not job-enhancing, but that doesn't prove that their absence will lead to progress. Teachers have often traded away greater on-site power for the comforts of solidarity as well as friendship. (They've left it to their unions to deal with that uglier power stuff.) Many teachers have been happy to work in isolation in part because it makes it easier to be supportive of each other in small, private ways while avoiding having to recognize uncomfortable differences. Avoiding controversy is second nature to such supportive relationships.

But schools, like good classrooms, are laboratories for learning the art of helpful criticism for kids and teachers, which includes bringing our differences out into the open. Since making sense of and dealing with differences is a central task of schooling—part of the meaning of being well educated—practicing it ourselves is a good way to pass it on to kids.

To practice the art of mutual criticism and disagreement requires, for starters, the same kind of trust we need from families: trusting each other's good intentions and reliability and then respecting each other's competence and capacity to improve. Learning to work this way together requires trial and error, over time—extended experience with each other at work. It doesn't happen quickly.

Building a culture in which it's counterproductive to create personal relationships that can't withstand necessary critical feedback is the challenge. There's criticism, and then there's criticism. Good editing is perhaps an apt metaphor for the kind of critical feedback we should be looking for. The point of a good editor's criticism is to see that what you want to say is well said. (Occasionally it's also to question what you want to say.) For schools, the equivalent would be criticism aimed at making sure a teacher's efforts are getting through to the audience, the students. The issue expands beyond the needs of an individual teacher—to the collection of classrooms that make up the whole. At stake is the ability to count on each other to work in ways that improve our own classrooms while keeping in mind the interests of the whole school—including what's happening to the kids across the hall. Inevitably there comes the messy moment when what one wants to say may be hard to say, and may even involve a central disagreement.

Small schools may make building such a culture feasible—in terms of our knowledge of and accessibility to each other—but I am too often reminded that putting it into practice is no easy matter.

How Teachers Work Together

I have discovered, from my experience, that going down the Colorado River on a raft (which I did one summer as part of an effort to build a professional community of school reformers) is a lot less trying than collaborating daily inside a school or school system. I barely anticipated this difficulty when we started Central Park East nearly thirty years ago. I figured we had the ideal lab for really showing off what trust and autonomy could do. We had all previously known each other as colleagues, believed we were on common ground, had chosen each other intentionally, and had unusual freedom to take up the challenge of starting our own version of schooling. But we ran into critical problems of trust within a year of opening our doors—and they almost sunk us. We began to wonder about each other's good intentions and felt nervous about whether we were telling each other the truth, not to mention having doubts about each other's competence! We were ill prepared for the amount of (unavailable) time it took to test out all our hopes and fears, and thus our ability to rely on each other wore thin fairly fast. We overcame these obstacles and reorganized, and CPE is healthier today, thirty years later, than it has ever been. Maybe some of the naïveté that led us astray is inevitable in the very act of faith that creating democratic institutions requires. And maybe the needed faith inevitably gets tested again and again over the long haul.

At Mission Hill I thought I had anticipated all the hurdles. (This was much like parenting, though, in that one doesn't necessarily make fewer mistakes with one's third child than one did with one's first.) This time we took time into account. We agreed, for example, that we would spend five hours a week together, above and beyond time needed for one's individual classroom, plus twenty additional professional days a year (fifteen over the summer). And to avoid feeling like martyrs, we would pay ourselves a decent stipend for this extra time. We also agreed to put money into smaller class sizes and assistant teachers so we could have a more comfortable workday.

It wasn't by chance, either, that I set as terms of employment an agreement to spend nearly half of that precious downtime together our very first semester taking a course with Eleanor Duckworth of Harvard University that had strictly to do with our own adult exploration of science—and we were joined by an equal number of parents. It was our form of a rope-climbing retreat, a way to build into the school the particular kind of trust needed to address our particular agenda.

The course had no direct practical bearing on our daily work—we explored the phases of the moon, mirror reflections, and balance. It required us, however, to publicly experience the confusions we felt when faced with a novel learning situation. It required us to make fools of ourselves. It meant we were confronted quickly with seeing what kind of distrust got in the way of our learning—a lesson for us not only in regard to the students we were teaching but also in terms of the learning we hoped to engage in together as adults.

I knew that trust also had to do with the question of who is in charge. Because of our status as a pilot school, we were able to have a clear formal governance structure. Our original agreement to open Mission Hill included a division of powers among staff, individual families, and the Mission Hill governing board that left the faculty with substantially more direct responsibility for the school's plan of work than was the general rule in most public or private schools. The collective staff responsibility for many decisions that generally rest with a superintendent or principal spelled out the need for a system of staff accountability.

Finally, we purposely organized the school to make tangible the idea that the kids belong to all of us. We first agreed that the entire faculty was responsible for knowing at least half the kids sufficiently well to take responsibility for all nine years of their education at Mission Hill. The standards for eighth grade work would thus belong to the teacher of kindergarten as well as the eighth grade teacher, as would decisions about whether a student met them. All teachers would sit on students' graduation committees and be advisers to seventh and eighth graders and eventually sign off on the quality of the work. Lots of other details followed—including the location of classrooms, the links between classes, and the role of colleagues in each other's professional decision making.

Having pushed the envelope this far, we could not avoid unpacking the conflicts between trust and skepticism on a small scale so essential to democratic life writ large. The devil, again, is in the details.

Becoming Critical Colleagues

Holding each other accountable starts with a shared and reliable knowledge base: good data—in the broadest sense of that word. The accumulation of formal and informal observations of student work, as well as of teacher-student interactions, is our primary base. At times, of course, the exchanges of viewpoint that such data provoke lead to the realization that we need more information, or a different kind of data, or more specialized expertise. Traditionally, this gathering of information, and laying out of hypotheses, is considered almost entirely the principal's job—or maybe the task of an outside supervisor or consultant. Much as kids think it fair to hide their mistakes from their teachers, so too do most teachers hide theirs from their supervisors. In turn, teachers traditionally rarely see each other at work, and certainly don't visit each other's classrooms unannounced. Information collected in this fashion, unsurprisingly, is unconvincing to those in the classroom, and rarely changes practice.

The question I put before us at Mission Hill that first year was, how can we take on the responsibility of learning from each other collectively; how can we go in and out of each other's rooms and get information, as well as give feedback—even tough feedback—about what we observe? How can we look at student work in ways that allow us to help our colleagues do stronger work? How can what we observe feed the schoolwide conversation? How do we put it together so that we can rethink our practices rather than just making each other uneasy? (Not unfamiliar questions for all teachers, although the setting for getting the answers might be.)

We've been tackling this, with growing success and many setbacks, for five years as I write this, and in doing so we've had to admit that it is harder than we imagined but also that it gets to the heart of what good teaching and learning is all about. No one sees any way out but going further in. There are two questions embedded in this process: what kind of evidence is needed, and what do we do with it once we think we have it? Both are complicated.

For example, am I interpreting what I see accurately? Would the teacher I'm observing recognize my description of her work? How can I get at what he's trying to do without sounding judgmental? Have we interpreted the mission or viewpoint of the school in compatible ways? How can we tell when the issue is poor practice versus poor theory? Have I missed a critical piece of background or context? What does the evidence of success need to look like? Can the evidence always be readily available—what about long-term side effects, unanticipated consequences? These questions bring us to the heart of those same five habits of mind that the school is dedicated to teaching kids. Overlapping coincidences like this one tell me that we're on the right track—that solving one problem will lead to the solution of others.

GATHERING EVIDENCE:

GETTING INTO EACH OTHER'S CLASSROOMS

Assistant principal Brian Straughter took on a study of staff members getting to know each other professionally for his doctoral dissertation, which imposed some useful discipline on us. We soon noticed that despite our declared intentions, our physical proximity, the presence of a second adult in each room, and our all-school curriculum themes, which lent themselves to increased collaboration, few people visited their colleagues' classrooms. The kids went back and forth often, and folks shared ideas, information, and resources in many ways, but little firsthand visiting occurred for long enough to make serious observations.

Staff members soon acknowledged that the reasons they didn't take advantage of all the supports we had put into place to encourage such observation and feedback were subtle ones. They were intensely focused on their own classrooms; everything else seemed as though it could wait—and wait—and being comfortable with each other made visiting seem less desirable, not more so. When Brian interviewed teachers for his dissertation, they acknowledged they were nervous when colleagues came in to observe their classrooms, as well as when they went into other people's rooms to observe. "Who am I to make judgments?" asked one teacher. The reticence was deep-seated. Running in and out and noticing things in passing seemed safer. Yet they all agreed that they had to overcome their reluctance to observe and critique each other.

Brian and I found we were experiencing the same feelings. It was easier to work with an individual student, to help out here or there. Observing a teacher suggested the need for feedback, and anything other than "I loved everything I saw" seemed risky. If I didn't get right back, teachers thought I had seen things I disapproved of. Any mildly questioning comment was blown out of proportion. In part it was my title, reputation, and expertise, and sometimes my tactless manner, that elicited such responses. But the volunteer consultants who hung around the school and who carried less authority experienced similar hesitancies. For myself, the need to get others involved was an imperative, because I knew that if I took the task on as mine, even if I learned to do it better, it would soon become part of my job description—and everyone else would be off the hook.

At first we set a day for teachers from each House—we call them the East House and West House—to exchange visits. This idea worked a few times. When Brian interviewed teachers, they said they would feel more comfortable if they could choose buddies they were already comfortable with to be their observers and could schedule time for follow-up later the same day. But many observers said they needed time overnight to think about what they had observed. Both ways were tried, but the practice petered out as a system by the end of the third year.

One lesson learned was that for regular observation and feedback to take place a supportive structure was necessary but was not sufficient in itself. As noted earlier, teaching, like parenting, involves acts of judgment that cut close to who we are, whether we are "good people" as well as whether we are competent people. Even with advance warning, it's hard to hide much. And the most neutral feedback ("this is what I saw") can hurt: a documentary film, after all, is not without its point of view. If the feedback hurts too much, we're going to build barriers that cut off the view.

Over these same early years, informal substitutes for the formal intervisitation system spontaneously developed alongside it, arising organically out of the structures we had created to get our work done. One teacher ordered a dry-erase tripod and placed it by her classroom door with a daily schedule and a question or quote for the day. Next, the teachers in the whole House had followed her example, and then the whole school was doing it, with barely a word being passed. One class built a carpeted stage where kids could read aloud or act out plays. Soon other classes did the same, and both Houses put stages in their half of the corridor. Thus was initiated not merely an architectural innovation but a sharpened awareness of the role of drama in the classroom. One teacher, Alicia, went to a workshop where she learned about color-coding children's books, and soon thereafter all the lower grades had adopted this practice—with Alicia's assistance. Another teacher, Geralyn, decided she needed many more blocks. Soon we had ordered enough for half the classes, but we were still short.

Regular House meetings, involving the four or five adults who shared responsibility for the approximately eighty kids belonging to the House, became an instrument for pushing the issues of feedback and accountability. "How did you do this?" "What can I do about Simon?" Some sharp criticisms were exchanged: "We agreed we'd follow this math sequence, and it seems you rarely do." The incentive for these interchanges was the transcendent desire to be sure the students you had or were going to have were being taught as best we knew how. Geralyn spent time in Kathy's room to get to know the kids she would be teaching the following year; she visited James's fourth and fifth grade class to see whether the way he was teaching math overlapped with what she was doing. These teachers disagreed on some key points, so all three then appealed to Ayla and Emily, who taught math to the oldest students in the House. What were Ayla's and Emily's expectations, and were those expectations reasonable?

Once a month the House meetings focused on a particular child of concern. What better way to consider the issues raised than to ask everyone to visit the presenting teacher's classroom to observe the student under review, as well as to look at examples of the student's work? Since everyone was studying the same curriculum, that too became a vehicle for actually looking at how the curriculum was carried out in each classroom. "How are you introducing *The Odyssey*? Can I come see?" "What are you doing about all the violence and sex?" The focus was shifted from observing each other to making observations about particular students, student work, and curriculum. The resulting criticisms, when they came, seemed more professional. Teachers found reasons to take over each other's classes occasionally, thus serving several purposes at once.

We agreed that colleagues would review each other's student progress reports. We canceled all meetings for a month so we could write longer narrative reports on each and every student, and we shared those reports with each other as first drafts and in the various stages of rewriting. We began to comment on each other's weekly newsletters and homework assignments—and we copied each other's ideas. In short, what Brian discovered was that the formal model he had begun with had been developed over many years to control the ways principals visit classrooms and was not necessarily the best model for our collegial and more intimate setting, at least not for gathering evidence.

WEIGHING THE EVIDENCE: WHAT TO MAKE OF IT?

Of course, the remaining question is how open and frank we are about what we don't like or are worried about. We may borrow here and there from each other, but are we talking about what shouldn't be borrowed? Taking good ideas from each other's newsletters is not the same as commenting critically on something you read, or even asking sharp and probing questions about a formulation, especially if we mean to be accountable to each other and the public. I soon realized, though, that some of the latter was occurring informally. Alphonse told me that Alicia had already made the same point to him that I was making about how to run certain instructional mini-meetings. He noted in passing how much Roberta had helped him work through a more in-depth curriculum; and Roberta in another conversation insisted it was vice versa. People's individual strengths became shared strengths. Over and over I'd hear casual remarks about what this person was learning from that one. Kathy had asked our volunteer literacy and documentation specialist, Brenda, to come in and observe her classroom and then pumped her for honest feedback. When I suggested that his morning meetings were going on for too long, James responded, "Actually, Geralyn made just the same point, so I know what you mean. I'm thinking about it," he added, "but I'm not sure I agree."

When some parents were being critical of one of our colleagues, I noticed that not only could I rely on my own judgment but that the staff as a whole had a range of data to help them decide whether the critique was warranted and also to suggest ways to be supportive—not just emotionally but professionally. Rarely have I been in a school where it seemed as reasonable to assert that colleagues were truly in a good position to know each other professionally.

It became clear that we had not only our own private opinions but the external and public data to talk about together with each other's work and the work of our collective students. These data came largely not from tests but from observations and actual student work, from the notes teachers keep on a regular basis and the folders full of ongoing student work. We also have a substantial collection of student work in our school archive—samples of writing, art, and research sorted and organized by student and year; we have five years of taped interviews of each and every student as a reader and their teacher's narrative reports. We have several years of final portfolios approved for graduation—with each committee's judgment of the student's work. And over time we hope to have (as CPE does) longitudinal data about what happens after students leave us. We are still novices at using this plethora of data well, partly because we are still learning how to use it and partly because we are nervous about using it. Will our conclusions erode or build collegiality? That depends, of course, on how we learn to define good collegiality, which in turn comes up against that familiar villain: insufficient time.

That using our knowledge effectively is harder than just obtaining it is hardly surprising. We must learn, or relearn, that openness to advice or criticism isn't the same as accepting it, and that disagreement isn't necessarily proof of being ornery or resistant to change. Teachers have long been used to being accused of "resistance" whenever they don't go along with the latest professional fad. Settling such issues by agreeing to let teachers do their own thing won't work, nor does adopting each new fad. It was important when Jim both acknowledged a colleague's criticism and also raised a question about its validity. Upholding disagreement as a bona fide stance is essential. Even with the best and simplest diagnostic test—in the hands of a doctor or a teacher—different interpretations are both possible and legitimate. It's then, when such differences surface, that the tough part begins. Two disagreeing doctors, looking at the same tests, may both be competent and still disagree with each other's diagnosis or treatment plan. So too with teachers. Determining what to do next—in both professions—involves providing a place to safely acknowledge doubt, to thrash out differences, try out ideas, revising along the way. Some differences must simply be lived with, and require acknowledging that judgments involve educated guesses and uncertainties. But sometimes a judgment must be made that what a colleague is doing is not okay.

Messy Differences of Opinion

One never knows for sure, of course, which observations will cause trouble. Alphonse, who takes the plunge quicker than most, insisted on discussing his hesitancy about hiring someone with very different beliefs—particular orthodox religious beliefs—which he thought might make for difficulties for himself and our students. Ayla's reaction, "I can't believe we're discussing this," stunned some of us into a moment's silence and confusion. But both Ayla and Alphonse persisted. Their tenacity helped us to achieve clarity and forced us to confront the natural tendency of a small, relationship-dependent community to hire only people "like ourselves." Facing this tendency, though, didn't dismiss the question of when beliefs might be irreconcilable. It made us ask, what are the boundaries between, on the one hand, the right of schools to stand for a coherent set of beliefs and practices and, on the other hand, an infringement of the school's responsibility as a public body? It also forced us to think about our own place in the group—what might endanger our sense of community?

Private and parochial schools don't need to worry about this question. They can afford to unabashedly declare themselves in ways public schools usually must avoid. The ubiquitous public mission statements schools and districts now publish are generally bland and full of interchangeable clichés for a good reason. Choice is often restricted to schools with different themes or trades: journalism, science, the arts. In contrast, private schools, like Catholic schools or the Waldorf schools, are frankly based on a set of beliefs and deep-seated philosophical assumptions that sharply distinguish them from other schools. Waldorf schools don't, on principle, teach reading until children have their first permanent teeth—although they don't deny that children could learn to read earlier. And they insist on working only with the finest tools and materials—no shoddy plastics for them—in precisely the proper way. That this is the right thing to do can be proved only if you accept the school's philosophical definitions of the good and well-lived life. Similarly, Catholic schools teach about Catholicism not because it's good for student achievement but because for believers it has a fundamental purpose that is larger and more important than academic achievement.

A few decades ago, public schools of choice were introduced as a challenge to the bland eclecticism of the one-and-only public school in town. A whole new set of issues arose. With choice in the public sector came the acknowledgment that "one size fits all" might not be true. Staff members didn't have to pretend the school was right for all families. Not all differences had to be papered over. But maybe some still did? Could you choose to organize around policies that led you to be all white or all black? Could you exclude kids with disabilities—or accept only high achievers or kids with "cooperative" parents?

A shared and explicit mission has its downsides. It poses issues that can be avoided in large, top-down, philosophically eclectic schools. In 1997, within a few weeks of opening our doors, virtually the entire staff at Mission Hill became aware that one teacher had a profoundly different way of running his classroom. It was an exciting classroom, and he was an appealing colleague. But he entirely ignored the agreed-upon schoolwide fall theme—the community of Mission Hill—and was building his classroom themes out of the interests that emerged in his class. The boys became interested in building airports, the girls in dollhouses. No one wanted to start our glorious enterprise with a fight, so we danced away from the conflict until—fortunately or unfortunately—the maverick teacher decided to quit. We had lost an opportunity.

Some teachers who generally stuck closer to the agreed-on schoolwide themes were nevertheless obviously just doing their own thing too: studying about dogs when we had agreed to focus on immigration. "Well," said Heidi, "dogs aren't native to America—they immigrated too." This rationalization became a school joke, but it also raised an important question about how our themes sometimes missed what really spoke to children's passions—their love for and curiosity about dogs, for example. This disagreement—once exposed—was healthy for us.

We differed over what a historical research paper should look like and what we properly ought to expect of a seventh or eighth grader showing off his or her skill as a budding historian. Should he be expected to have a viewpoint, weigh primary evidence, be aware of different viewpoints, make connections—or should he first just get the information straight? Teachers accustomed to setting their own class standards found that the need to agree on these expectations put them into conflict with colleagues in uncomfortable ways.

Although they agreed with what the school brochure said about teaching reading and writing—using methods that come closer to the way children learn their first language rather than teaching discrete skills—the teachers of our two classrooms for five- and six-year-olds interpreted this approach in somewhat different ways. Alicia set aside more all-class time for the formal phonics than Kathy did, and she worried sooner about kids who weren't early readers. I wondered whether it would be useful to sharpen the issue or to let it go and see what happened. One day, however, Alicia made a formal presentation to the staff about an exciting early literacy institute she had attended. The institute's approach differed from the school's largely in terms of the amount of time set aside for exclusively literacy-based activities.

As she was passing a proposed schedule around to show how it might work, someone asked how it fit in with block building, artwork, or thematic topics. I chimed in with some questions also tinged with worry, and implicit criticism. Alicia stopped us. She said it was hard for her even to go on; she felt disrespected by our response. We heard her out. In the ensuing uncomfortable discussion over how this presentation had been handled, we stayed away from the issue of the potential incompatibility of the approach Alicia was presenting and the existing school practices and beliefs. We all felt terrible and withdrew from tackling the important—if nuanced—differences that she had brought to our attention, and that could have been sources of strength if we had known better how to tackle them.

Many issues get harder to handle because we are also dancing around questions that are perceived as particularly sensitive—race and gender above all. While these issues are critical enough to warrant a separate chapter, it's sometimes hard to know when one conversation is driving the other. Some of our apparently strictly professional disputes may well have race-sensitive implications that are too often covered up out of the best of intentions, as well as the worst of our fears.

Here as elsewhere the line between disagreements that are important to talk about in the interest of improved practice and those that distract a school from its agreed-upon mission are not easy to distinguish. Someone recently reminded me how I had resolved a disagreement over special education at Central Park East (CPE) many years ago. Some teachers had announced that they wanted to discuss whether kids with special needs belonged at CPE at our spring retreat. I ruled this question as out of order by saying that CPE was founded for the purpose of serving all kids and that as a public school we had no choice. I thereby declared it undiscussable. The friend who recalled the event described it with admiration. I felt pleased, but I was also aware that the explosive underlying issues didn't therefore go away; by prohibiting the discussion, I had perhaps missed a way to bring the issues out of that subterranean underground. Still, it was also important to draw a line, to assert our core beliefs and public obligations clearly. Would it be okay to discuss whether we were open to kids of all races?

A school that is always rethinking basic premises creates unacceptable intellectual and moral disorder for kids and families. Sometimes it's even worth sticking with the wrong consistencies for a while. In schools, as in classrooms and families, there are necessary routines and rituals. No one has to claim that theirs is the only way or legislate their methods for others to follow. But "this is how we do it" is not a mere random choice either. Whether the issue is whether students wear uniforms or how we address each other, we like to mark our turf. How we do so, however, is usually symptomatic of our values and beliefs, although it is not definitive. The power to invent our own distinctions is critical. Schools that brag that they are a replica of a standardized model—one more McDonalds—are less able to powerfully influence their students than those that take pride in their shared consensus that "this is the way" we do things here. It may not matter that kids call their teachers by their first name at Mission Hill, but the youngsters rarely describe the school without mentioning it with pride.

Caution is also required because we have all had very little, sometimes virtually no, experience with face-to-face democracy—so some of our efforts are clumsy out of sheer inexperience. As with us, so with our kids. And it's important to remember that our perceptions, accurate or not, of our own power affect the way we feel about exposing our differences. As the power differences between us and our students make honest exchange hard, so do they too among colleagues. For some, a colleague making a face or appearing in some way to dismiss an idea can be a conversation stopper. For others, this is the moment to dig deeper—"so? do you disagree?" Some of the Mission Hill staff feel put down by what I think of as just a useful provocation, raising a possible alternate way of thinking (which I myself may not even agree with). A friend of mine recently claimed that my more contentious style derived from my entitled status as a middle-class white person. Surely class and whiteness helped. Although I had felt more different from most other middle-class white girls than like them when I was growing up, having a greater than average sense of my rightful place probably helped a lot—even if my family tradition told me I'd also have to fight for it.

Facing rather than avoiding conflict appears time-consuming up front and doesn't always come with a happy ending. What is at stake is deciding how important it is to take one's ideas seriously enough to insist that they be heard. It's sometimes easier to complain about an unfair system than to be a powerful member of a tough profession. When I feel frustrated, I remind myself that the same spirit is what's needed to be a powerful member of a tough society. On my most discouraged days I think what we're trying to do is probably impossible, but then I think that it's surely no more impossible than the dream of democracy writ larger. It's a work in progress.

The Payoff: The Educative Value of Teachers Struggling with Trusting Each Other

How we as teachers deal with these dilemmas is relevant to what we teach kids, and what kids will take from us for life. In the exit interviews Brenda conducted with our first crew of Mission Hill eighth graders, she was startled by one comment she heard over and over: how much—sometimes students felt it was too much—the school had held them responsible for their work, had insisted that it was "up to them," had not coddled them. They expressed in equal measure appreciation for and irritation with the demand that they had do some assignment over again—"it's not right yet; try again." They found assuming this responsibility both exhilarating and difficult. A few complained that they didn't have "real" classes and didn't learn "real" stuff like most kids do. But they said we were always there when asked to be; they knew we wouldn't refuse to give help and almost never put the need for help down to laziness or dumbness. Not coincidentally, this sense of power—that they, in the end, were the ones ultimately responsible for what they did with the opportunities offered—is the outcome of the culture the staff was building for itself. What students learned was the same thing we as teachers were learning: to be accountable for ourselves and for each other.

We believed that even letting kids know that we as teachers sometimes disagreed with each other, and that we sometimes disagreed with their families, was useful (within bounds). Kids usually know when quarrels arise among those they depend on, but they less often have a chance to observe them being dealt with respectfully and, even if not resolved, being handled so that work can go on. The advice from family systems experts to have children attend family conferences stemmed from the evidence they had gathered that most kids had far worse fantasies about adult differences than the conflicts that surfaced when we confronted issues together. The youngsters also discovered, in the process, that sometimes we changed our mind if they presented convincing arguments and evidence.

The central purposes of schooling are deeply embedded in learning how to do exactly what it was we were struggling with among ourselves—taking responsibility for being well informed, developing our own ideas, enjoying the power of ideas, being open to the views of others, and learning how to talk about tough and often sensitive stuff in an informed and persuasive way—including disagreeing with each other. Taking responsibility for oneself and one's ideas is not a bad shorthand definition of being well educated. So becoming skillful at getting the relationships right for learning among the faculty, and learning how to be both critical and appreciative of each other is not a distraction but the core of what kids can learn from keeping company with us.

Some of the best serious discussions we have with kids are at moments of disagreement between adults or between adults and kids. They seem less afraid of strong disagreements than we are, and opening up alternate views is usually exciting to them, like the time some fourth and fifth graders were happy to miss lunch and recess to argue with each other—and James and me—about evolution, God, and damnation. While we all enjoyed it, James and I also saw skills and knowledge displayed that we had not seen before. Showing kids what a culture of debate might look like ought to be a function of democratic schools. But James and I were both thrilled and nervous—at the healthy passion and skill being displayed, as well as the Pandora's box we might be opening. What would parents say when the discussion was described that night at home? Kids are unlikely to learn to handle such sensitive issues in intellectually useful ways, however, unless airing and discussing differences of opinion are part of the everyday culture of the adults around them, not a rare and scary exception—or something heard only on talk radio. Urban Academy, a member of Ted Sizer's Coalition of Essential Schools (CES) in New York City, begins virtually all its courses with adult debates—the livelier and more contentious the better.

The staff laugh at me for a passionate argument I got into with my eighth grade advisee, Akwasi—right in the middle of the office—about how best to represent his ideas in graph form. Geralyn wondered, only half jokingly, "How many adults would be willing to take Deb on that way?" Akwasi was perhaps showing off the nature of the trust that he felt toward the school in this public way. Sometimes the kids may lead the way.

CHAPTER FIVE

Trusting Each Other's Agendas and Intentions: The Dynamics of Race and Class

In this country, American means white. Everybody else has to hyphenate.
—Marian Wright Edelman, 1992

My colleague Brian and I were walking down the block to my car when five-year-old Derek came bounding out of the school with his grandmother. He called across to me with breezy familiarity, "Hi, Deborah." Before I had a chance to reply, his grandmother admonished him to call me "Miss Deborah." I responded, without thinking (intending to reassure her?), that it was okay to call me Deborah. As we sat in the car, Brian, who comes from a traditional African American family, noted that this had probably not been a wise response and may have left the grandmother feeling she had been admonished and Derek feeling confused. Having grown up at a time when adults were always addressed by their last names, I was not unaware of the issue. Yet there was a difference. How I was addressed carried less weight for me than it did for Brian and many other African Americans. It was this, in turn, that had made it seem less awkward when the younger staff at Central Park East decided, in the late 1960s, that it would be okay for kids to call us by our first names. Besides, my own children's friends were by then also calling me by my first name. I was, in short, far less sensitive to the nuances than was Brian, who in fact insists, for various reasons, that students call him Mr. Straughter. He caught the culture clash—and its possible racial, class, and generational implications—which I had barely noticed, or perhaps had mis-construed, especially the power of putting "miss" in front of a first name, which wasn't part of my tradition at all.

In a diverse society, divided in many often unacknowledged ways by race, class, ethnicity, and more, such mishaps may have deeper repercussions than they would in more homogeneous cultures, and above all in less racist ones. They are not unconnected to how kids learn—and to what extent kids and their families trust the adult company their children are keeping.

Not every colleague would have felt comfortable correcting me as Brian did, so I need to find other ways to learn, and schools need to be places where such learning can occur. We can't wait until we have reached a common consciousness regarding issues of race, gender, so-cial class, or other differences. We can't wait until we have good reason to trust everyone we need to. We have to tackle all these and more in the here and now—as we go about teaching the kids to line up, do their math, write their letters. We have to do it even though in so many ways we will still be distrustful and wary of each other. Having spent thirty-five years teaching in schools where my background and that of the vast majority of my students differed in myriads of ways has thus been full of mishaps.

I acknowledged early on that earning even limited trust would be no easy task. I also learned that a family's need for schooling for their kids would lead most to some form of tentative—if just for today—trust, and many to far more. But I also knew that many sent mixed messages in the safety of their homes. Everything over and above the most provisional forms of trust would be, I decided, a bonus—deserved, I hoped, but not to be counted on. I have only to take into account my own suspicions regarding the trustworthiness of those different from me to imagine, for example, the depths of suspicion and rage that many black Americans must struggle with every day. What's surprising, I sometimes think, is how often these emotions don't overwhelm everything else, not how often they do, and how often people do seem to extend their trust beyond any reasonable measure.

The issues are not only personal—and they are that—but also social and institutional, often beyond our individual control. When racial tensions combine with class distrust, their ferocity is terrible to behold—as they did in 1974 when Boston's elite were perceived as trying to integrate other children's schools—without sufficient thought about what would be needed to make the integration work in their own children's schools, or in 1968 when several well-intentioned New York City foundations used their power to initiate an experiment on behalf of more local school autonomy in several predominantly African American communities, leading to a long and bitter teachers' strike. Such conflicts—which resonate with America's long history of race and class conflict—make talking about building trustworthy schools in which adults and children learn through a myriad of often informal relationships seem utopian, absurd, romantic. I'd agree if it weren't a fact that the boundaries of race and class are overcome time and again, despite compelling reasons for distrust, in schools across America—even if this isn't the norm. Such schools do not merely survive an uneasy truce, but kids often thrive in them in ways that they might not in a more homogeneous community. In short, heterogeneity (also known as integration), for all its problems, is good for us. These schools work even though the people involved have not overcome their fear of each other, even though they have not wiped out all hostilities based on race or class.

My immediate responsibility was to give all kids as good an education as I would offer my own children, but without assuming that the children I taught, or their families' dreams for them, were, in all respects, like my own. They never are. (Even our own children are often not quite what we imagined them to be.) And some are more unalike than others. But they are also—and this was critical to remember—never so different that I couldn't figure out ways to be useful. Empathy never requires that we actually be alike in every way; in fact, it is based on the assumption of difference.

Our differences are not only problems but also potential assets. They require us to learn more deeply and powerfully, precisely because we are obliged to step into the shoes of others, to see the world from more perspectives. That's one of the values of a diverse student population and a diverse staff—and a diverse society. Tackling differences is not just for the sake of fairness or antiracism but also for just plain good education. While it may have once been feasible to imagine living as though one's own tribe were the only one on the face of the earth, the only group that needed to be seriously encountered and understood, one can't deal with any of the issues we face today, from the most local to the most international, if one holds on to such an egocentric view. (The term *multiculturalism* once popularly described this idea, although it is currently a casualty of the political correctness of a more conservative time.) Stepping intellectually, socially, and morally into the shoes of others is a central part of what it means to be well educated today, and thus it is not a side issue on the way to teaching the multiplication tables but is of equal if not greater importance and requires at least as much intellectual rigor.

Mission Hill's Work

For us at Mission Hill, the issue of difference that predominates in the lives of students, parents, and teachers—though it is not the only one, for sure—is race. Much of our self-conscious collective work has addressed issues of race, often with partial, precarious success. Having a strongly antiracist statement of purpose and even a multiracial staff—both characteristic of Mission Hill—doesn't resolve anything; although it's good to have both. But neither of these gets at the informal agendas we harbor.

A few disproportionately white activist families tried to organize a parent discussion around race the first year at Mission Hill. Some parents of color felt that while the effort was probably well intentioned, it was inappropriate. It fizzled, leaving everyone uncomfortable. However, it produced a parent group called Circle of Color, which offered some families a place to explore their dreams and fears and led to a race-conscious policy by the Parent Council with regard to parent representation on both the school's governing board and the leadership of the parent council. But family discussions about race were not pursued.

Our schoolwide study of ancient Egypt during our second year raised issues of how many black and white Egyptologists interpreted race in ancient times differently and reminded us how race sometimes influenced our understanding of historical facts. It provided a way for race to be discussed on a different level. We spent a lot of time that year and the next on race and racism as we all worked on the details of the schoolwide American history themes, including approaches to the peopling of the Americas, and the African American experience. We tangled over teachers' different ways of helping kids tackle the brutality of slavery—particularly in regard to playacting plantation life or master-slave relations with young children, which often came across as insensitive and carried wounding messages. We brought in experts, and we listened hard to each other. Similarly, in studying the U.S. Constitution, we debated how much attention should go to the racism of the times and how much to its democratic impulses. Some of the differences that arose were political, but some stemmed from how we have experienced life in America. So it went with topic after topic. The following year, faced with responding to the correlation between race and standardized testing, I suggested we discuss the work of an African American Stanford psychologist, Claude Steele, on race and the testing gap. The ensuing presentation of Steele's ideas met with more silences than discussion. Maybe, Ayla said, we wouldn't be ready for this until we spent more time tackling how race influenced our relationships with each other. We agreed to try it and hired facilitators to help us.

We started with the "easier" stuff—putting our feelings about who we were on the table. We stuck with hearing and acknowledging them rather than delving into what they meant for us professionally. Next we broke into affinity groups, whites in one group, people of color in another. Two teachers' decision to create their own temporary biracial affinity group was apparently accepted comfortably. I had difficulty with the whole process, as I have had before at such consciousness-raising sessions. In part, my reservations are like those that make me avoid the retreats I described earlier—where one is expected to share secrets and explore private fears. But I'm also uneasy with the premises underlying this black-white notion of identity. It clashes with my own deeply entrenched anxieties about where being a Jew fits in—having been raised at a time when "racism" was synonymous with anti-Semitism. Even today "the white race" is frequently a shorthand for white Christians, excluding Jews as much as Asians, Arabs, or Africans.

Exploring rage and guilt over white privilege is one approach for bringing difficult issues up front. But getting to the next step—where people grapple with the differences they hear, where not all opinions and experiences are deemed okay and yet no one can lay down the correct answers—is tougher. It has increasingly seemed to me that possibly that first step is beside the point for the purpose of building a school—to doing something about our teaching practices. But I'm not sure, given how important it seems to some of my colleagues. I twist and turn, looking for the dividing line between useful versus useless staff discussion—where private rage needs to be explored and where it needs to be avoided, and where and with whom such discussion should take place. We did some of the difficult exploration of identity, and then we put it on hold and moved on to tackle our own teaching practice.

We agreed that racist words or actions—even unintentional or arguably misinterpreted ones—that affect our students and families are not private voluntary questions but rather central to school talk. Addressing these questions is an obligation that comes with membership on the teaching staff. We needed, after all, to direct our colleagues' attention to all behaviors we think inappropriate to a strong learning environment. Our personal struggle with racism, anti-Semitism, feminism, and so on can be private, but overt manifestations of bias affect kids and families. (Homophobia, we learned, is probably as tough to deal with in schools as racism—sometimes tougher.) But what our students and families, and the public, need from us is not for us to overcome all our biases but for us to be willing to look closely and carefully at how our attitudes and assumptions affect our teaching practices. We struggled to make such self-awareness a regular aspect of our conversations—observing how particulars have differing effects on the kids before us, even, for example, on learning to read and write.

Above all, this is needed when it comes to race, where American schools have such a particularly appalling history.

Looking at the particulars was provocative and interesting; we noted that certain uses of language, even in math problems, as well as ways of handling discipline or dress codes, carried messages that were not always obvious. This closer examination meant acknowledging and taking advantage of the expertise within our immediate ranks (staff, kids, families), as well as looking to outside experts (books and consultants). Differences of opinion existed between experts—including some with equal credentials and similar personal backgrounds—and judgments needed to be made after hearing varying viewpoints.

One teacher's use of Jesse Jackson as an example of how we are all flawed (at a time when he was on the front page for personal misconduct) might have been insensitive, racist, or useful. We didn't all see eye to eye on this one. We knew the answer depended on who and how and when; no fixed rules were possible, but it was important to bring our sensitivities out into the open. Of course, we always knew it helped, when possible, to discuss these teaching strategies with colleagues and families ahead of time. But teaching doesn't usually allow for that. Could we accept the fact that mistakes themselves could—as in the study of science—be educational for kids and teachers if we dared to use them that way? There's more danger in avoiding sensitive subjects than in occasionally making blunders. It was hard to hear that books and favorite stories I was raised on—like *The Five Chinese Brothers* or my family's oral version of the children's picture book *Tikki Tikki Tembo*—were offensive to some Asian families for reasons I had never had the opportunity to examine. *Examining the reasons why they were offensive led to an expansion of my knowledge of history and culture—an opening to new thoughts, not a closing of my mind on old ones.*

I notice occasionally that some white parents flinch when a black teacher refers to "our children"—clearly meaning not theirs. Do some black parents flinch if white teachers use such a phrase—and do they wonder who is "ours"? The "ours" used by black and white teachers may be parallel grammatically, but they have a different history. The special protectiveness that black teachers extend to African American children is hard for me not to honor. Is there a place for questions about this kind of issue? My instinct, where the feelings run deep (and where time to discuss anything is always so hard to find), is usually— "don't touch." But that's an instinct that needs to be challenged, if not every time it comes into play, more often than even I—known for being confrontational—am accustomed to.

Even the debates over how to teach reading or math can have overtones of racial conflict, as Lisa Delpit and others have noted. Differentiating when our disagreements reflect a difference of opinion versus a question of racial perspective is touchy. Is phonics a race or class dispute, a right versus left debate, or a theoretical difference about how language is acquired?

And to what extent are we each so individually different, shaped by so many different forces, that even generalizations intended to undercut racism—the kind of cultural observations that proliferate in some well-intentioned antiracism workshops, such as "Latino children avoid looking adults in the eye" and "black boys need fast pacing"— should make us uneasy. Certainly we need to be wary of how easily we can slip into such generalizations even as we seek to overcome other ones, and how sometimes they can become excuses for expecting less or backing off from being tough where toughness is needed. I'm not expecting to ever feel completely at ease about any of these issues, but "easier" is a great relief—and I keep my fingers crossed.

Impact on the Teacher Culture

There is no school I've worked in where teachers—regardless of other commonalties or differences—didn't have their own private codes, unspoken signals, and unacknowledged differing agendas when it comes to issues of race and ethnicity. While there are sharp intragroup differences as well, there are those moments when all teachers of color become dead silent in the middle of what appears to be a lively and friendly discussion. Or when a member of a racial minority closes up or walks out over something her white colleagues have no clue about. People probably clam up because they think what they say will be misunderstood—or sometimes because it's too exasperating and time-consuming to explain "once again." We may move a little further into understanding where we're coming from, what caused the tension, but we never move through and beyond it forever. After one of our more intense efforts to delve into race at Mission Hill, we were all feeling edgy. At first we didn't even make the connection between our discussions about our racial identities and the palpable tension and long silences at our usually jovial staff meetings. Finally one white teacher suggested that her sense of underlying tension was rooted in her acute awareness that whatever she said might be interpreted differently by her colleagues of color. Possibly her black colleagues were thinking—"about time." But at one such meeting a black colleague blurted out to a white colleague, "Take a chance. Say what you think. I can take care of myself"—or words, as I recall it, to that effect. It seemed to me a corner turned.

Just as parents have doubts, so too do teachers: Can white teachers truly understand kids of color? If not, what harm might they do? I no longer think this fear can be wiped out by "trust"—as I perhaps once did. But I think that like other issues of trust this question can be coped with provisionally. The answers lie, as these first few chapters suggest, in a climate of sufficiently open debate and discussion, so that at least some of the often unnoticed messages teachers send children about the privileged status of white culture can be both raised and countered. The presumptions of whiteness are unavoidably a part of many of the books assigned and read together—whiteness is, after all, taken for granted as the norm of our mainstream American culture. Of course, in part the simple personal relationships that we build with each other soften the impact of our mistakes. Watching each other at work eases most fears and replaces them with affection and respect over time.

Still, even when we care, the division between whites and teachers of color crop up in unexpected places and may need attending to. When Central Park East Secondary School debated whether kids should be allowed to wear hats in school, for example, the African American teachers were more likely to be against the hats; similarly, the appeal of intimate rural settings for school retreats seemed at times to reflect a racial divide. Who among us felt more or less in need of bucolic remoteness (and maybe even private bedrooms and bathrooms) varied, it seemed, partly by age but also by race. Was I inventing an issue? Should the disparity go unnoted, or should it be addressed? By whom? I decided, as I more and more have, that what I notice—even if inaccurately—should be said aloud—although not always then and there.

We recently had a session about difficult family conferences, how to get stuff out in the open that might be worrying us or a family. I had invited in a friend of the school, a highly respected white family social worker to talk with us. An undercurrent of resistance and lack of openness was present throughout what was, I thought, an excellent presentation. I had no clue. Afterward an African American colleague told me how angry she had been that we had had a white outsider lead the discussion, given that most of our families were black. She said, "I felt erased." Whether she was right or not, I was annoyed that it hadn't seemed obvious to me to bring it up.

So, how to survive in our native land? Is there no end to these complicated interactions? We probably need to accept an incompletely enlightened coexistence—with occasional rough spots. If three black teachers gather to talk, are they talking about "us" whites—and does the same hold true in reverse? And so what? White teachers need to become less uncomfortable knowing that teachers of color (like parents and kids) on occasion check out whether what they saw, heard, or felt was just personal or racial. How safe am I here? How am I being perceived? This probing is what I rely on other Jews for on occasion, and other women frequently. The need for such "checking out" has never left me, especially if I wanted to push the agenda, exercise my own powers, take some risks. Would he or she have said that to me if I were a man? I ask a friend (as I quietly seethe at what appears to be male condescension). What to do about it, even if it's true, is another matter. We need at the very least to be aware of the forms of entitlement that interfere with the collegiality of our discussions, the assumptions about who holds power and how those who hold it exercise it, the kinds of power that go unnamed even with all our rules and principles.

Power in and of itself is hardly the enemy. We're trying to teach kids, after all, how to examine and enjoy it, both the power to do important, even risky things, as well as the power to influence and direct others. (In both these senses of power, being white comes with entitlements that are much harder won by those growing up black in America.) And my own particular advantages in my school—my status as principal, my ability to access political and fiscal resources, not to mention the knowledge and skill that come with age—are powers that have been useful to us and hardly ones we want to give up. But they make certain claims on my part to equality more problematic. Power—of all kinds—can be trusted or distrusted better when it's brought out into the open. Keeping company with kids includes exposing them to how power works.

There are other significant forms of collegial empowerment at work in a school. Teachers new to the school as well as new to teaching are not sure what power to assume and what not to. They bring habits developed over a lifetime lived in largely hierarchical institutions, habits that shouldn't be expected to disappear because of our more egalitarian working rules. What's for real? they wonder. When does Deborah really show her true colors—and insist on getting her way? Even I don't know the full answer to this question. There are all the other "minorities" we carry within our head—not always as visible as race: the "injuries of class," so powerfully written about by Richard Sennett and Jonathan Cobb (*The Hidden Injuries of Class*), the wounds of centuries of assumptions about women's mental incapacities, our gender identification (being gay or lesbian), being Jewish or Muslim in a Christian world, being fat in a nation that makes a fetish of thinness, being one or another kind of dissenter politically or religiously, or having always been loners and oddballs. Each of us has his or her own history of having been hurt and excluded and labeled that needs to be examined as it affects the here and now of our school. Such self-examination will help us each figure out how (not just whether) to trust the school and our colleagues, and in turn how to use these insights into "otherness" as aids in teaching our kids. Our curriculum —the literature we introduce, the speakers we bring in, the trips we take, the topics we select, the language we use—encompasses the many ways in which power and otherness are experienced.

If we are keeping company with our kids, we can't avoid the subject of race with them; it's part of the work we do and the stuff we study. Besides, the kids desperately need to be able to talk about it openly with the adults in their lives. Otherwise it becomes an unmentioned game between teachers and kids—as kids sometimes use the issues to avoid facing the tasks before them. Pretending that race isn't part of our school's culture probably doesn't fool many kids; but worse, it's dangerous. And what better place to start that talk than among the grown-ups?

We need to see ourselves as a self-conscious community of learners, engaged sometimes, to use Saint Augustine's words, "in heated arguing . . . to spice our general agreement with dissent," as discussed in chapter 4—but being sure we keep the difficult subjects on the table. It takes being able, as Brian did, to share an insight with a colleague without pointing a finger. That's hard enough to do with any of our practices, but of course it's a capacity tested to its full when we're dealing with sensitive issues. As we observe each other, do we notice patterns—whom we interrupt and whom we wait out, how we praise different work, who gets to play which role in plays, what issues of language we attend to or ignore, which experts we turn to? Do we look at each other's homework assignments and ask ourselves how particular assumptions and language may increase the gap between children of middle versus lower class, black versus white families? What is it that some teachers know and do that makes them more successful with certain kids? Rather than viewing these questions as burdens, we could view such discourse as exciting, interesting, challenging. The trust that needs to be built between teachers around race ultimately depends on our getting to that point—at least some of the time.

All of this is an argument on behalf of being "data-driven." While many, in these days of tough, businesslike jargon in the school world, see the phrase as strictly a question of counting and measuring, for us it also requires looking for the evidence in the stories, the artifacts, the long-term outcomes of our work—what happens to our kids. The particular situations and scenarios, with all their rich detail, need to be documented with care. But this, after all, is the stuff teachers naturally enjoy talking about. We keep detailed notes and records so that we have the anecdotal stuff to share. All of this is hard to do, but it ultimately depends on us cultivating our teacherly fascination for details, the kind that allows us to respond to our own and children's cognitive mistakes with curiosity—"I never thought of it that way!"—rather than with praise or blame.

Such an approach means being mindful of the ways our behavior can narrow or widen the distrust that a racist and classist society necessarily engenders toward those in positions of power and status—which includes teachers. As long as "us"—the people in power—by connotation excludes people of color (unless otherwise explicitly noted), schools in America may always seem to belong to someone else—even perhaps when they are run largely by teachers of color! How the exclusion occurs is often hard for most of us to see. It's built into our language and cultural images, ones shared to some degree by whites and blacks alike. I know I am often literally tone deaf—or merely number?—to what kids hear the world saying about who counts, who matters.

It takes conscious, even unremitting, effort to create communities that resonate equally for people of color. Listening more closely to ourselves and allowing ourselves to be more carefully listened to might go a long way to change the messages that we unintentionally pass on to kids about the color of the world. As Theresa Perry, a noted African American educator and author, noted in a talk she gave at Mission Hill, there are things about a school that tell you whom it belongs to from the moment you walk into the lobby. Many of these things remain for me still elusive.

*   *   *

I did not become a teacher in order to solve problems of inequity and racism. I became a teacher because I happened to fall in love with my first (definitely temporary, so I thought) job as a kindergarten teacher. But it has not been entirely an accident that I have taught in largely black or Latino schools and school districts or happened to live in such communities. Nor is it an accident that I assumed that the task for me, as a teacher, was to figure out what it was about the work that could make a powerful difference for the kids I taught, whomever they might be, and how that was affected by the inescapable fact that I was white and most of my students were not, and that I was middle class and most were poor, and that I was Jewish while most of my students were Christian. Pretending it didn't matter would deprive me of knowledge I needed.

I'm still as fascinated as I was the day I began teaching in Beulah Shoesmith School on Chicago's South Side by the details of how each and every child learns to put together the meaning of his or her own world. But I am more conscious than I once was of the role race and culture play in how children put together that meaning, and this awareness has in turn influenced and enriched my own way of seeing and experiencing the world.

PART TWO

Testing and Trust

CHAPTER SIX

Why Tests Don't Test
What We Think They Do

Attempts to substitute counterfeit science for individual judgment not only lead to failure, and at times major disasters, but also discredit real science, and undermine faith in human reason.
—Isaiah Berlin, 1996

The culture of the small schools I've described so far—with all its complexities and possibilities—is threatened every day by the rampant spread of standardized testing and standardized curricula in schools today. We are witnessing a radical redefinition of the task of public education, driven by the widespread belief that by focusing our attention on externally imposed tests we can both produce higher achievement and restore public trust in our schools. I will argue that quite the opposite is true: the increasing use of standardized tests both undermines achievement and increases the distrust we have for teachers, students, and our own judgments. Some schools and some communities—especially privileged ones—can treat testing as a game and continue to do their own thing (if they don't get caught up in annually outdoing their rivals). But for those schools at the bottom to start with, the new regime of standardization is deadly medicine, with no redeeming virtues. To fully understand why it's dangerous to base schooling on standardized testing, we need to look at the tests closely. We need to see what they can and cannot do—and why more and better ones are not the answer. We need to see how in all their varied guises they run directly counter to the kind of intellectual work being proposed in the schools I've described and the kind of relationships of trust that underlie the culture of such schools. Finally, we need to explore alternatives to testing that serve its legitimate purposes but that are more consistent with an education for powerful citizenship.

Growing up in the thirties and forties, I was not exposed to standardized tests—or if I took any, the scores were kept secret. Some kids took the newly invented SATs if they wanted to get into an Ivy League school. But since I was going to a Midwestern college, I didn't even take those. Still I wasn't a test doubter. In 1964 I eagerly supported neighborhood and civil rights activists, including two longtime friends, Ann Cook and Herb Mack, who stole secret test data from the Chicago public schools' central offices to prove the system's racism. We were right about the racism, but we were wrong in thinking that tests would prove for long a useful tool in reversing it.

The modern testing enterprise was designed as a response to the novel idea that trust could be scientifically defined. While standardized testing has an ancient history, it is only at the turn of the twentieth century that interest in what came to be called psychometrics revolutionized the world of standardized testing. Originally designed to objectively classify subgroups by IQ, and thus steeped in the racial and class biases of the time, standardized tests were seen a half century later as a way to undermine such biases. They appeared to some to offer an objective and thus possibly a more trustworthy way to determine true merit than the judgment of teachers and counselors. Behind the increased interest in standardized testing for school uses was also a reasonable and in fact responsible skepticism: a demand that schools have ways to show parents and citizens that their increasingly important judgments of students were unbiased—beyond the corruptions of power and prejudice.

By the 1950s there was increasing interest in using testing as an opportunity to crash the gates of gentlemanly bias—to overcome quotas developed to keep some people out and others in. If we could rely on the industry's new scientific claims, how much easier it would be to make educational decisions, sort kids into different educational tracks, and make selections for special programs. As Nicholas Lemann's book on the SAT, *The Big Test,* chronicles, the Educational

Testing Service would be able to choose more fairly among applicants for Ivy League colleges. In the sixties and seventies, such tests became the centerpiece of a movement for accountability championed by civil rights activists in K–12 schools. They were focused now on school-based achievement but were designed by psychometricians to match the same criteria that went into IQ tests and SATs, which presumably measured a quality—"aptitude"—that would not change over time (although, ironically, the early national Head Start program, where I taught in the mid-1960s, used IQ tests, not achievement tests, to track student and program progress). Many African Americans in particular, who had good reason to think that their children were not only misserved but also misjudged by subjective racist standards, hoped that such tests would both undermine the bias of largely white-led school systems and focus attention on the inequality of the schools that served their children. Objective data, they hoped, could push the agenda for change.

At the heart of the psychometric design were two key and appealing words: *reliability* and *validity* (as well as the bell curve, also known as the normal curve—a particular rank ordering of scores that was deemed by many scientists to be nature's way of distributing most of life's characteristics). Think for a moment about driver's tests. We all want a driver's test that's going to be the same from one day to the next and that is not dependent on who happens to be the inspector for your exam. That's what is meant by reliability—the score will be consistent no matter where or when you were tested or who tested you. But we also want to be sure that what is tested has something to do with real road skills—a test that on the face of it covers a fair sample of the agreed-upon most critical skills, and also that predicts pretty well whether you're a safer driver than someone who fails it. This is what is meant by the term *test validity*. These qualities are arguably important in a trusting relationship too—you want to be able to count on your friend to be the same person today as tomorrow, and you hope that the things you count on her for are important and will stand the test of time. (Although note that in neither example above are we concerned with rank order or bell curves.)

The inventors of such tests were thus grappling with how to make trustworthy and fair decisions, just as I am. They claim nearly a century ago to have found the answer. It's this claim I want to examine in this chapter.

When a parent of a sixth grader tells me that her child is reading on a 4.8 level, I want to know what to tell her about how trustworthy this information is. I know she is torn between trusting her own judgment, the teacher's, or the test's. If they don't agree, she has been told by state authorities that the latter is the "real" answer and that both of the former are biased. The same dilemma increasingly bedevils teachers as they make decisions about promoting a student or awarding a diploma—when the results differ, whom to trust?

It turns out that there is substantial technical unreliability in test scores—what is called "standard measurement error." Given this margin of error, there's a very good chance that a score of 4.8 really falls anywhere between 3.8 and 5.8, even assuming there has been no unorthodox coaching, cheating, or test maker scoring errors.

But what if there is a deeper problem than a margin of error—the test's reliability if given on another day or scored by a different scorer? What if—in addition—what is being measured on reading or math tests (or any of many other standardized achievement tests) is not the level of a student's skill at reading or doing math but something else altogether?

What if the road test, to return to that analogy, were "reliable" —you did as well on one day, or with one inspector, as the next—but it did not measure what it means to be a good driver? What if the standardized achievement tests we use in our schools cannot produce what they appear to promise and have built-in biases and errors at least as deep as our ordinary human ones—and more dangerous precisely because they appear to be so objective and unchallengeable.

Suppose such tests cannot produce scores with the accuracy of even the average routine medical test. Then our belief that we can sidestep the fallible judgment of our fellow citizens—parents and teachers—is both fundamentally misguided and actively harmful. Then our kids are losing schools designed to place greater weight on the judgment of adults for no good reason, and decisions not only about their own individual fate but also about curriculum, pedagogy, and even the very definition of what it means to be well educated are being made on the basis of a flawed instrument. Keep this in mind.

As long as we think tests can come close to the claims they make in terms of reliability and validity, it seems reasonable to ignore mere subjective human judgment. But if the claims I'm making in this chapter are accurate, then sooner or later we'll have to get on with inventing those fallible but trustworthy-enough institutions I've been describing. Many critics of standardized achievement tests are, in other words, not just romantics who place academic goals below affective ones, softies who don't want to face tough truths, utopians waiting for a perfect measuring tool, or just defensive whiny educators who can't bear to be held accountable or to be tough on kids. They're not against science or rigor. In fact, I believe that the critics include educators with the highest standards for kids and for the power of kids' minds.

My History with Tests

The first time I bothered to look at a test with any critical scrutiny was when my own bookworm son did badly on his third grade reading test. It was in figuring out what he did wrong that I first encountered the possibility of two right answers—his and the test maker's.

That same year I began teaching in Harlem and had the chance to create a small kindergarten-through-third-grade cluster of four classes. Now was my chance to prove that all children could learn. When the first group reached second grade (when testing in New York City began), I expected to be able finally to prove my point. I was startled to discover that many children who I knew were reading well did not score well. So I became a scholar of reading tests. My son, it turned out, was just one small example of how these tests could mislead us.

I tape-recorded hours of interviews with young children in which we went over parts of the reading test together. (The results were published in *Reading Failure and the Tests*, City College, 1973). I discovered that there were students who could read the stories with oral fluency

and discuss the contents intelligently but would chose the wrong answer. Reading skill helped—but not a lot. They rarely did better when
I read it all aloud to them. Pressed for the first time to justify my right
selections against the logic of an intelligent and self-confident seven-
year-old, I found I had to run next door occasionally to be sure I was
right. The students' answers were based on experiences, interpretations, and associations that would not have occurred to me yet seemed
eminently reasonable. Here are some examples (from tests still widely
in use twenty-five years later, although the items have, of course,
changed slightly):

> Some days I should stay in bed. Today was one of those days. "Good morn-
> ing," Mom said. "Don't you have a clean shirt to wear? That one looks dirty."
> "Sam," said Dad, "your shoes are on the wrong feet." I got dressed all over
> again. By the time I ate breakfast my cereal was soggy. Then I stopped, as
> usual, for Bill. He was not home. He had already gone to school. I walked
> there alone. When I got to school, Bill yelled, "Here comes Sam, the snail."
>
> Question: Why was Sam so slow in getting to school? (a) He overslept. (b) He
> had to get dressed twice. (c) He fooled around. (d) He did not like school.

Most of the children said "Sam was fooling around." Some chose "he
had to get dressed twice." A few said, "He probably didn't like school
and that's why his friends called him a snail." But not one had trouble
reading the passage aloud.

There were other children who arrived at the "wrong" answers because they were using a kind of logic that the test is not designed to tap
or accept:

> An architect's most important tools are his (e) pencil and paper. (f) building.
> (g) ideas. (h) bricks.

Most children selected (e) pencil and paper. The few who picked
(g) knew something the others didn't, but no amount of drill and
practice, whether in phonics or "whole language," would change
their minds.

> A giant is always (e) huge. (f) fierce. (g) mean. (h) scary.

The correct answer (having trouble?) is "huge." But the kids who
picked one of the others had no trouble reading and using all four
words properly.

Choose the word that best completes each sentence. A sage individual is
(5) touchy. (6) old. (7) testy. (8) wise.

Mark selected "old." He was annoyed when told the answer was "wise." That would make a silly sentence, he insisted.

Finally some selected the wrong answer because they did not possess a specific piece of information that is not part of the general store of knowledge of all second graders.

The frequency of a sound determines its (1) treble. (2) pitch. (3) volume.
(4) harmony.

This question tests knowledge of physics, not the ability to read well in English. You can know what frequency means in a nontechnical sense perfectly well and still not know that sound travels in waves and that the frequency of a sound wave determines its pitch—especially if you're in second grade.

In this respect, as in others, these tests are remarkably reminiscent of IQ tests, which also depend upon a consensus about what is reasonably part of every testee's culture and prior understanding—of language, context, the way things work. I recently took a 1905 IQ test given to immigrants on Ellis Island, only to be classified a moron.

As a favor to a friend I allowed one of my sons to take a more modern IQ test. My friend reported that he did well on advanced items involving abstract reasoning but very poorly on earlier items regarding social conventions and commonsense reasoning. He failed one, for example, that asked him what he would do if when sent to the store for a loaf of a particular kind of bread he discovered that the store didn't sell that brand. He gave the lowest-level answer: "I'd go back home." The higher-rated answers included "I'd try another store," and "I'd ask the storekeeper to help me select something close to what I wanted." I knew why he didn't choose either of the other answers: he wasn't old enough to cross the busy New York City streets to try another store without permission, and he was too shy to talk to strangers.

I tried out one of the IQ questions on my own students at school, and discovered that they were penalized for similar "faulty" reasoning when asked what they would do if they lost a friend's ball. The low-ranking answer was "tell my mother," the middle-ranking was "just apologize," and the high-ranking was "buy him a new ball" or "give him one of my balls" or some other form of restitution. In fact, on a whole series of questions that differentiated between children who turned to authority rather than worked out a principled and independent response, kids' answers largely depended on their family's social class position and completely reversed what my own observations suggested they would do in real life. "Tell your teacher," not "figure it out yourself," is the refrain poor children had heard from family and school for years—even if they didn't always obey it. How were they to know that this time—for this test—they were to ignore that refrain? In IQ tests, as in virtually all so-called achievement tests, children's social experience and language, as well as what they believe the testers want them to say, influence their answers in ways I had not anticipated.

For some kids it is an idiosyncratic quality—their tendency always to think outside the box, to see themselves as somehow different —that handicaps them, like my son. But for many others, their communities are outside the box, nonmainstream enough to turn an apparently simple item into a tricky one. Life experience counts. That Hemingway's works are written on a fifth grade readability level does not mean they would be well understood by most eleven-year-olds, who have not yet had the experiences that make the stories intelligible.

Even when children were not baffled by the subject matter, they still often missed the testers' logic for selecting one answer over all others. For reasons I was slow to understand, there was always at least one answer that even to me seemed almost right, misleading, or tricky; these answers are called "distracters." While at first I thought this an obvious place to seek reform, it turned out these were a necessary part of the test design.

Norm-Referenced Tests

My discoveries in the late sixties didn't do much good. We were in the throes of one of New York's reform periods, with the sole goal of raising test scores. For the next five years we were cajoled and threatened. The black community's anger over the 1967 and 1968 teacher strikes, and the civil rights movement, then at its height, helped fuel the demand that all kids should be able to read on grade level by third grade—as defined by a test score of 3.7 in April (the seventh month) of third grade. Newspaper editors, school boards, aroused citizens, and politicians clamored for higher standards and an end to illiteracy. Why, they complained, do half the kids always test below grade level no matter how much money we pour into their schools? Why do scores go up for a time and then bounce back to where they were before? Why can't everyone read on a third grade level by third grade? Is that asking too much?

Few were the citizens, even educators, who knew that scores, in the long run, on these kinds of tests do not change. No matter how much the children collectively improve, half always score above and half below "grade level," by definition. The scoring system ensures this result, a practice achievement tests inherited from their forebears—IQ tests.

Demanding that more kids get higher scores on standardized tests—be they IQ tests or achievement tests—is, under these circumstances, something like demanding that students line up faster so that more will be in the front half of the line. Even seemingly modest demands, that all high school graduates read "at least on a tenth grade level," are statistically nonsense—unless we change labels or the way tests are designed (more on an attempt to do that in the next chapter). When the Lake Wobegon effect (Garrison Keillor's fictional town, "where all the children are above average") appears statewide or nationwide, we are in effect simply misreporting scores. This is sooner or later "cured" by renorming, so that the scores will once again mean what they say they mean—where each examinee stands with reference to all others of his or her age or grade level, or at least to the norm group mean. For a time, of course, while the same test is in use, scores can and do generally rise. And, when the tests are renormed, it is sometimes possible through a method called "equating" to compare scores on a new test to those on an old one. But in real life, when the scores drop back down, it's some hapless superintendent whose neck is on the chopping board, spluttering away to no avail about renorming.

Therefore—and this is worth emphasizing—scores are not statements of competence, no matter how much we try to label them so afterward. By design, 50 percent of the students' scores will fall below the median—and 50 percent above. This would be true no matter what the competence of the population actually is. By definition, scores on these kinds of tests can never inform the public as to whether better learning and better teaching are taking place. Whether, as a group, children in America are fabulous readers or lousy ones, the test will always put 50 percent on top, because it is based on a sample presumably accurately representing all children of this age and grade. It would be absurd to ask all the nation's kids to score in the top 50 percent in the name of high standards, just as it would be absurd to demand that all the teams in the American league have won-lost records above .500, on the grounds that surely they play better baseball than the teams in the minor leagues, where the average of won-lost is also .500.

This is roughly how such tests are created. The pool of items (and multiple answers)—however they are originally gathered—are first checked out on a representative sample of students of the grade for whom the test is intended. Each item's level of difficulty is found. Scores are compiled and rank order established, with some tweaking here and there to ensure that the items differentiate properly and produce a rank order—ideally a bell curve, which is presumed to be the natural distribution of human traits. We can argue until we're blue in the face about whether all kids "ought" to know enough to be in the top 25 percent, but the scoring ensures that only 25 percent of a representative population of kids of that age will get enough answers right to be in the top 25 percent. Psychometrically good items properly differentiate kids; bad items don't. Items that everyone would get right, for instance, aren't useful, even if it turned out that they constituted what professionals believed to be evidence of appropriate third grade skills. When we "beat" the test, the test maker is simply obliged in time to go back and renorm the test. If everyone's scores are rising, so will scores of a representative sample. The test given to a new sample, and a new norm—that is, a new median score—will be defined at a new point, and we will be back where we started with respect to score distributions.

If scores begin to bunch up, or some questions do not provide useful differentiation (if everyone gets them right, for instance), test makers are obliged to go back to the field and redesign the test—so that it once again differentiates properly—maybe adding more difficult passages or problems, or devising trickier and more complex ways of wording the questions with subtler nuances or some other fix to get the same distribution. Even just different alternate answers—those distracters referred to earlier—to the same questions will serve the purpose. It's interesting to note that the percentages of right or wrong answers vary enormously depending on what alternatives are offered. We know who the sixteenth president of the United States is or isn't, as Thomas Guskey reminds us in a wonderful article in *Phi Delta Kappan,* depending on what alternatives we are offered. By a small change of wording, we appear to be either knowledgeable or ignorant—so we can keep the curve intact.

Isn't it amazing that we have for nearly a half century been promoting a way of measuring school success with an instrument guaranteed never to be able to tell us if we are achieving that goal? Designed after a system serving a very different purpose—ranking people according to some supposedly fixed aptitude—standardized tests are utterly counterproductive for the educational purpose of seeing what kids have learned in school so as to improve education for all.

Why Coaching Is Not Okay

A good pretest sample, the normed group described above, is built on the presumption—which test makers take as a demonstrable fact —that there are predictable differences between children based on their characteristics in terms of race and gender, as well as where they live, their family's income, and so on. The sample, if it is large enough and properly drawn, works pretty well—although as with all forms of sampling there is measurement error. Only if sampling assumptions are right will test scores be reliable and remain usable for sufficient periods of time to justify the cost and time involved in the development of psychometrically reliable instruments. Other factors can contribute to measurement error as well. One reason that test makers have always been so concerned with secrecy is to ensure against item contamination based on too much specific prior knowledge—which can range from plain cheating to "good" coaching. A high score based on a high level of coaching is probably not as accurate a predictor of the real-life competence of a testee, which is after all what the test maker hopes the rank order can predict, as a high score minus coaching. Why not? Because the promised connection between the two—score and predicted competence—was based on a sampled population that was not coached. But do we want high scores or scores with validity—and which do we want more? We seem to have settled for the former.

In my early teaching days the only pretest coaching allowed was a one-pager handed out by the testing company and administered under strict conditions the same day the test was given. The test makers' manuals warned that any other coaching was cheating and would invalidate the results. In my youth, even SATs were given with absolutely no preparation—just a couple of number two pencils and a ticket of admission to a big anonymous testing center. Then came the PSAT—to prepare kids for the SAT, and today coaching for the PSAT and the SATs demonstrably boost scores for those who can afford it.

Today coaching is encouraged starting with five-year-olds. We are asked to teach to tests like these as soon as our children enter school—and sometimes earlier, to get children into the "right" nursery school. But it is crucial to understand that these kinds of standardized tests are meant to be given without coaching. As we saw, any rise in scores will simply shift the norm (of course, not immediately). But for the same reason the tests' predictive value is threatened—a raw score of sixty-three no longer means that a child is in the seventy-fourth percentile. The coaching, furthermore, is focused not on what's most important—but only on what will show up on tests. These tests don't pick out knowledge that everyone should know if they're well educated; rather test makers pick questions that will provide the proper spread of scores. The goal in picking questions for these tests is not the same as a teacher's might be. These are tests designed to sort people, not to evaluate how well the teacher has taught or how well the students have learned, a point that cannot bear enough repeating.

Whether tests happen to be called aptitude tests or achievement tests, they are actually much the same thing. The SAT acknowledged this when it decided to change the name from Scholastic Aptitude Test to Scholastic Achievement Test without making any other changes in the test itself. The trouble is that there ought to be a difference: a test designed to capture something innate ought not to be able to measure something schools can teach. In fact, both (I would claim) are testing something that is largely social and cultural—with biology and schooling adding their minor influences.

The task of the test makers was to create a test as impervious as possible to the impact of schooling while still being credibly connected to the kind of learning valued by schools. In *The Tyranny of Testing,* published in 1964, Nobel Prize–winning physicist Banesh Hoffmann described his correspondence with one test publisher, who explained to him that even the correctness of an answer (however desirable) was not actually the fundamental criterion. The wrong answers that Hoffman discovered on a well-known physics test could, he pointed out, actually serve the purpose just as well as—and in fact better than—the right answers. The test publisher did not defend using such items, but only asserted the irrelevance of the criticism in terms of the score's statistical credibility—the students who answered the offending question the way the test makers preferred were the "right ones," the students with generally higher total scores—even though it was the wrong answer.

I have argued, in short, that the kinds of standardized tests advocated for improving education are designed with no such goal in mind. They are designed for sorting students, and will relentlessly do so, to the frustration of those who call for improving the performance of all kids on standardized tests. And they will frustrate attempts to use them as goals for teaching: they are not meant to be taught to.

But there are other questions to raise. Let's turn to look at the question of bias in tests: the inevitable tendency of such instruments to discriminate against members of some subgroup—with or without coaching.

Bias in Testing

Test validity requires a fairly clear preconceived idea about who the good students are—those likely, all else being equal, to do well by other criteria—including future life success, school success, or success on other tests now or in the future. Most reading tests use other reading tests as well as IQ tests as their external validation. The granddaddy of psychometric testing—IQ tests—originally used their subjects' occupations as the external standard of validity. If doctors got more items wrong and plumbers got more right, the choice of items was not doing its job. (Read Stephen Jay Gould's *The Mismeasure of Man* for the whole story.) The SAT claims to use success at college freshman-level work as validation (but not the year after college, and not life success at all). Since women get better college grades even as freshmen—and lower SAT scores—the validity of the SAT as an indicator of being ready for even college courses seems questionable.

Test makers, like opinion pollsters, must also check the internal consistency of their items by using a statistical procedure that yields a "coefficient of correlation." This is a technique for finding out whether the specific items in a test are measuring the same thing rather than being indicators of one or more variables. Other procedures take this process to an even finer level. But some note that in fact what this technique does is discriminate against subgroups whose pattern of answers varies from the dominant high scorers'. These are issues opinion pollsters also worry about. Pollsters have long been aware that an item might be intended to pick out the strength of one variable, but if respondents are interpreting the question differently based on another variable entirely, real validity has been sacrificed. We saw this principle at work in the test items described earlier—as seven- and eight-year-olds reasoned their way through a reading test. If the group affected is small enough, these kinds of mistakes are easier to ignore, but they can still cause considerable trouble for this or that individual, and above all for this or that subgroup.

Any choice of subject matter, vocabulary, syntax, metaphors, word associations, and values presupposes a certain social and personal history. We may have equally big vocabularies, but different ones. We may be speaking a grammar that is consistent and accepted, but not the standardized one used in academia. I'm probably good at guessing the right answers because I have been steeped in the subculture—vocabulary and grammar at the very least—upon which test makers build their system, and I am sufficiently trusting not to look much deeper than my first guess (unlike my son, who seemed to look deliberately for the unexpected answer, as though he imagined he'd have the opportunity to argue with the scorer!). Of course, vocabulary and grammar are but a small part of what I'm steeped in. I do not have to figure out what the test makers might want me to think, feel, or say—I've subliminally tuned in to the same world the tests are tapping. As in the case of a *New York Times* crossword maven, the right answers are lurking right beneath the surface—until you try the crossword puzzles of a different elite. Try doing British ones! When I was preparing for the National Teachers Exam in my midthirties, I recognized for the first time that my natural biases might not work for me on a test. My schooling history had not been mainstream. So I had to engage in a more cautious and self-conscious process before filling in the boxes. At any age, being outside the culture the test is designed to tap imposes a handicap. At the very least, the need for such intellectual caution slows handicapped "outlander" testees down. At the very most, it utterly baffles them.

When bias was first raised as a testing issue, test makers obligingly changed some rural scenes to urban ones, darkened some complexions, and eliminated a few archaic terms. (Today they include literary excerpts from far more nonwhite authors, for example.) But the victory was irrelevant. For the tool requires a definition of being well educated, and such a definition presumes being inside one particular favored culture. Our backgrounds do discriminate between us to the advantage of some and the disadvantage of others—even on such mundane matters as making sense of a math problem or a reading passage. Even simple phonics tests depend on agreement about the pronunciation of words that in fact vary by dialect. Pin and pen. It is hard to know, for that matter, exactly what it is in an item that makes it easier for some people than others to get the "right" answer.

Let us consider an example from a reading test I encountered some years ago:

> The children lived in a pleasant tree-lined street. One morning trucks came and chopped down the trees in order to widen the road for a new 4-lane highway. When spring came, the birds and squirrels, who used to live in the trees, did not come back.
>
> The question: When the truck came, the children felt (a) excited. (b) silly. (c) sad. (d) angry.

How was it that I immediately knew the right answer was (c) "sad"? In real life, of course, children—rich or poor, black or white— are unlikely to feel sad at the arrival of trucks, especially if they don't know what is going to happen next. Yet somehow I knew we were supposed to feel sad when the environment was going to be damaged and intuitively picked the right answer without carefully examining the text or the logic of the alternatives. Experience had taught me to trust my intuition. And indeed this item, while it actually penalizes careful and accurate reading, worked much as it was supposed to on the children in my school. Nonreaders failed. But otherwise it mainly differentiated children of one background from those of another. Since experience has taught us that differences in class background often also correlate with greater reading fluency, we seldom question the reasonableness of our responses. Only when a pattern appears that interferes with prior accepted predictions—the kids I expected to do well didn't —is a red flag sent up.

In this case a few boys insisted: why wouldn't the children be excited? How did they know that they were going to cut down the trees anyhow? Only then did I reread the question and catch the bias. It is a bad item, but like Banesh Hoffmann's items, it did its job of differentiation.

The bias is in the nature of the tool. Any standardized tool in which neither the test taker nor his teacher is allowed to exercise human judgment—to explain, justify, adapt for this or that kid's particular background knowledge—carries such bias. It is necessarily steeped in prior cultural assumptions—norms—that favor some kids over others. This is not a question of test makers having anything against any particular group of test takers; the nature of such tests requires that they distinguish between those who are in and those who are out. The test must discriminate and rank order on some basis. If all testees responded the same way, the question would be a bad item; if the "wrong" people got it right, that would also make it a bad item.

Unfortunately, the task of overcoming such implicit life norms —whether undertaken wisely or not—requires far more effort on the part of some children and communities than others (as I discovered when I tried to teach kids to get right answers), even if the tests are never renormed. And the effort to teach kids to get the right answers adds to the social mistrust that makes overcoming the odds harder in the end by undermining some children's intelligent, natural responses with paper-thin school-learned alternatives. Our coaching at Central Park East Secondary School actually lowered some students' SAT scores; as they became more anxious about tricks, they ignored their own good sense when it was right as well as when it was wrong.

For children, as for adults, not knowing what others take for granted is embarrassing, and silencing. It makes some children, and some adults, more and more hesitant to raise their hands, to show off their smartness, out of distrust for their own thought processes. If school classrooms are often risky places to expose one's uncertainties, then the testing room is even more so, as Claude Steele shows in an insightful series in the *Atlantic Monthly* ("Thin Ice: 'Stereotype Threat' and Black College Students"). For many people, an externally imposed test is the example par excellence of dangerous territory, a place where the clues are few and far between regarding the trustworthiness of the questions or their authors. The kinds of tricks and traps that are a game to some represent grave danger for others. Steele describes a series of experiments to demonstrate the susceptibility of the most successful African American college students to self-doubt in the face of tests. Tests are above all threatening to kids who have strong academic skills but for whom this represents what Steele calls a "stereotype threat": being asked to prove they aren't what others think they are. Steele presents a complex argument, but he shows that a similar effect is at work when white men are consciously pitted against Asians on math tests, for example. Thus, he argues, such test scores misrepresent actual achievement for those who are the objects of negative stereotypes. The very pressure to overcome the stereotype depresses scores rather than improving them. While Steele's work was focused on African Americans, it's likely that something similar affects Latinos.

The social distrust that lies behind this reaction is not paranoia. Life experience strongly confirms for most young people why such distrust is appropriate. In a society in which one out of every three young black and Hispanic males is likely to spend time in prison as a result in part of similar stereotypes, distrust is a survival skill.

The standardized achievement test that probably carries the greatest weight in the lives of American students is the SAT. We know that the statistics on SAT scores have been devastating to black racial self-esteem. African Americans have consistently scored more than a hundred points below white and Asian Americans, and often this gap is used to make some political or educational point. Close study regarding how these results occur has not been undertaken—including just asking white and black students (as I did earlier with my second graders) to explain the differences in their answers. Only close examination of how the questions work for the students can uncover what unintended biases may be at work.

Princeton Review analyst Jay Rosner notes that the makers of the SAT have detailed information, as do all testing companies, by race on all pretested questions. He has uncovered a number of items that the Educational Testing Service has pretested on which nonwhites outperformed whites, some items that showed very small gaps by race, and others for which the differences were vast. Decisions regarding which items to use would, Rosner calculated, produce enormously different results. This puzzler needs far more attention. It corresponds with my own classroom and schoolhouse experience—that social, racial, and ethnic histories play a huge difference in what seems hard and easy, what wording complicates and what wording simplifies. Selecting items with this in mind can compound our racial biases or undermine them; so how these choices are made needs explication. At present what lies behind such decisions is part of the mysterious black box of test design.

Here is one of the examples of a vocabulary item that Rosner uncovered.

Fill in the blanks:

The actor's bearing on stage seemed _____;
her movements were natural and her technique _____.

a. unremitting, blasé
b. fluent, tentative
c. unstudied, uncontrived
d. grandiose, uncontrolled

Black respondents chose "c" (the right answer) 3 percent more frequently than did whites. Who knows why? Nor do we know why whites choose right answers on "white preference" items, or why some are or aren't chosen. One might assume this sort of discrepancy couldn't happen in math; but it does.

Try the two questions below.

If the square root of 2x is an integer, which of the following must be an integer?

a. square root of x
b. x
c. 4x
d. x squared
e. 2 times (x squared)

If the area of a square is 4 times (x squared), what is the length of a side?

a. x
b. 2x
c. 4x
d. x squared
e. 2 times (x squared)

While these look to this layperson like they are getting at not only equally hard but actually the same knowledge, the first one is answered right more often by black students and the second more often by white students. What assumptions determine how many questions for which differences are small versus large to include? Are these known results even considered? Should they be?

During the years I worked with high school students, I was frustrated over and over by the fact that otherwise less competent white students regularly did better on the SAT than the top African American kids at the school. Our school's performance-based portfolios turned out to be far better predictors of college success than the SAT, although no doubt they too had their biases.

Both Claude Steele's and Rosner's work suggest that the strictly racial differentiation in the SAT results may be exaggerated by such factors. Something similar may be true for class and economic differences. Things unrelated to intelligence, poor schooling, or a family's educational deficits may be at work.

I note the SAT precisely because, regardless of its faults, we're unlikely on the K–12 level ever to have tests as scrupulously designed and highly scrutinized as the SATs. If such problems arise even in the SATs, what can we expect of tests designed on the cheap and in a rush to meet the high-pressure needs of this or that state and locality for more and more massive testing, tests that must change often (in some cases annually, once thought an insuperable obstacle by reputable testing firms) to avoid the pitfalls of cheating and overcoaching? When careers and life opportunities are on the line, to expect such instruments—in the hands of ordinary human beings to boot—to merit all our trust seems unreasonable.

To organize schooling around tests is a blow to serious intellectual work; given that no particulars are likely to merit more than one or two questions, and deeper and subtler thought is often an impediment to scoring high. Reading a lot of books on a subject can actually leave one more baffled when confronted with a request for just the two most important causes of the Civil War, or one of the best reasons for Hitler's rise to power (answer on a recent Massachusetts state test: "the

Versailles treaty"—an appalling answer except for the fact that the alternatives were less reasonable). Letting schools become focused on coaching to test items is not just silly—given their normed character—but counterproductive to the aims of good schooling—which should include looking behind the alternate answers offered, not becoming good at intuiting "the one right answer."

Neither their academic skill at performing appropriate second grade tasks—like being able to read!—nor their intelligence in making reasonable connections and assumptions was the main stumbling block facing my seven-year-olds in the early 1970s. The same is true for the high school seniors I tried to prepare for the SATs fifteen years later and the fourteen-year-olds I try now to get ready for the Stanford 9's or the Massachusetts Comprehensive Assessment System's annual tests.

None of this seemed quite so unfair when we were more frankly trying to sort children. What small minority—the tests once asked—should go on to high school or college? Which kids should be shunted off to "special" schools for dummies? The test could be "trusted" to help counselors and admission officers make the socially reasonable decision, the odds-on favorite. No one intended to change the nature of schooling or the life chances of whole subgroups of children when this kind of testing was invented in the early part of the last century. If kids were rich enough, it didn't matter how they tested, because they could likely buy their way into good schools. It mattered most to the less wealthy who showed sufficient schooling promise to go on to an elite prep school versus a less elite one, who might be placed in a gifted class rather than the normal class, who might be accepted into a private school or leave school altogether or go on to a vocational or comprehensive school. Nor did the tests seem so unfair when we accepted as obvious that class, gender, and race had a natural and inevitable relationship to school ability. Tests were designed to pick out the unlikely gem amid the rougher stones. Race and class biases were so deeply a part of the culture of the educated elite that their biases, which today seem flagrant, were unnoticeable then. Today it is both unfair and inconsistent with our proclaimed goal—to educate all children to tackle advanced intellectual work—and our equally pro-claimed insistence that we have no biases.

So? What to do?

If this analysis is correct, we cannot trust such tests to determine an individual's competence or the success of any particular school, school district, or state, not to mention the merit of any school reform or set of reforms. We can win occasional short-term public relations victories for this or that program by improving testable skills, but in the end such victories will be at the price of good education. Scores will rise and fall as superintendents come and go; that's the way the game works. And meanwhile we distort the education we offer as we try to beat the game. The injury falls heaviest on those most depen-dent on the school and those whose scores are more likely to be low. A quick look at what's happening in our schools today reminds us of how much the tests determine the kind of schooling kids receive. If the tests are bad indicators, it follows that the pedagogy and curriculum designed to raise scores are bad pedagogy and bad curriculum.

W. James Popham, emeritus professor at the University of Califor-nia–Los Angeles and an eminent psychometrician, puts it this way: "An achievement test would seem to be measuring what students have learned in school. But this is not the measurement function of tradi-tional standardized achievement tests. . . . In short, 'achievement' tests really aren't. And because many of their items measure what students bring to school, not what they learn there, traditional standardized achievement tests should have no role in evaluating our schools."

Is there no alternative? In chapter 7 we'll examine one effort to cre-ate an alternative built around psychometric testing principles, with a critical difference: no expectations of a bell-shaped curve and no re-norming to ensure that the curve stays the same over time.

As Jacques Barzun argues, while "an objective test of mind is a con-tradiction in terms, . . . a fair test, a searching examination, a just esti-mate are not." What the more substantial alternatives all combine are some of the same elements that go into any reliable and valid system of assessment (with the usual meaning of these words): attention to providing multiple perspectives and opportunities, ways to correct for bias, an array of different forms of evidence including some more traditional standardized testlike formats, the availability of public exposure and critique, and a broader time frame versus a single snapshot. Such alternatives would also distinguish between an assessment system for measuring individual kids and one for assessing a school or system in which sampling is a far sounder approach. The answers may not be as easily captured, of course, in a front-page headline or graph or rank-ordering.

Our misfounded faith that everything can be reduced to the precision of some of the hard sciences and math leads sensible and otherwise compassionate psychometricians and politicians to foolishness. They are left to conclude that they must rely on test scores to make decisions, even when they themselves acknowledge that real-life hard data suggest it is wrong to do so. This is what led the commissioner of education in New York State to insist that in spite of their verified successes, thirty-seven high schools—like the ones I founded in East Harlem—be discontinued unless they use state regent's test scores as evidence to show that their students had been successfully taught. The rigorous system of public portfolio reviews that these thirty-seven schools pioneered, and which turned out to be such good predictors of real-life success, failed because they didn't meet the requirements established for standardized norm-referenced tests! Tests became the definition of success, not merely a predictor of it.

If the purpose of schooling is to improve our judgments, then the tools we use to measure our work might, in fact, be best thought of in the same terms. There is no reason to abandon these good English words—*reliability* and *validity*—whose dictionary definitions are as good as ever, just because they were also adopted for a narrow technical meaning a century ago. That the tests we've been examining are not in the end very reliable or valid in our sense of these words does not mean we shouldn't seek to build schools that honor such ideas. To be well educated is to become more sensitive to the kind of data we ought to trust, to how much reliability we should require, and to what forms of validity lend authority to one or another's claims to truth. We need to play with all the definitions of trust we've been exploring to build systems of accountability that serve such goals. Since tests can't definitively tell us whether and how well Johnny can read, we should return them to the status of being just one more mildly interesting piece of evidence among many.

CHAPTER SEVEN

Standardization versus Standards

P roponents of the current so-called standards-based reform, including state and national government leaders, business leaders, and editors of most of our leading newspapers, claim that the way to restore trust to public education is through objective tests. They argue that it is possible to design tests that can stand the weight of accountability, make high-stakes decisions, direct good teaching, and tell everyone where they stand in relation to everyone else—and define what it means to be well educated.

The search for such a good test—one that gets around the difficulties posed by the norm-referenced tests, and that can be used not just to measure but also to drive school reform—keeps us tied to a false hope —however well intentioned.

One can see the appeal, however. Reformers of all stripes have always hoped there was a way to do this. Design a test with norms based on what people should be able to do, not just the range of how they currently perform, more like a driver's test. Wouldn't it make all our jobs easier if we could find a way to get everyone to measure themselves against an absolute standard of what it means to be well educated? Then wouldn't this help direct the changes we want in schools (and society) and focus our attention on the acknowledged weak spots? Even if people didn't at first agree on our definition of the standard, wouldn't most people go along simply out of the desire to do well? The test would do the convincing. That's what standards-based reform is about—making change happen, raising our sights.

The purpose of this new wave of testing is not, remember, to obtain more data, but to change the schools. We already have more standardized, objective, and centrally collected information than any country on earth. We have test scores of every sort at every age level, broken down every which way you can imagine—race, class, gender, geography—plus data on attendance and dropout rates, much of which goes back half a century or more. (We've known for decades that no neighborhood high school in the Bronx graduates more than 30 percent of its incoming ninth graders.) But the trouble is that such measures, while they spot where there's trouble, don't at the same time solve the trouble. That's the new idea: testing *as* reform, not *for* reform.

The popular new drive to hold schools and school reform accountable to test scores has many appeals. It's built around the idea that the villain is mostly low expectations and a failure of will power. Since both are indubitably factors in failure and less onerous to tackle than poverty, for example, this notion eliminates victimology. And it keeps us focused. Ordinary citizens, including parents and teachers, are aware of how often local parent councils, teacher unions, principals, and local school boards have abused their powers—here's a way to catch them. No more excuses. The more objective the standards, the more distant and scientific the results; the more universal the population tested, then the more nonnegotiable the consequences, and the less room for argument, excuses, flexibility, bias, and compromise. In a society in which adults often feel helpless to control their students or their children, even to know them, this approach has additional blessings. It appears to avoid the issue of trusting anyone: one's kids, their teachers, their schools—or oneself. It is, we are told, also more like the merciless but efficient and effective marketplace—with test scores standing in for the bottom line. And for this reason it also appeals to those who have the most reason to distrust our schools: urban minority families and those inclined to be suspicious of any public institution. Finally, a tool with teeth, one that offers both clear and universal goals and direct observable consequences for not meeting them.

The idea of holding schools accountable to test scores has its attractions, fits aspects of the national mood, and adheres to a long-standing American tradition of turning to standardized testing as the answer to our ills. But the trouble is, as we keep relearning generation after generation, it contradicts what we know about how human beings learn and what tests can and cannot do. That a standardized one-size-fits-all test could be invented and imposed by the state, that teachers could unashamedly teach to such a test, that all kids could theoretically succeed at this test, and that it could be true to any form of serious intellectual and/or technical psychometric standards is just plain undoable. And the idea that such an instrument should define our necessarily varied and at times conflicting definitions of being well educated is, worse still, undesirable.

The So-Called New Test

In the late nineties, states sought to impose newly designed state curriculums—keyed to, or in some cases interchangeable with, a set of agreed-upon standards—by way of tests. This development made more obvious the essential contradiction between a testing system designed to be secret and normed to fit a bell curve—and the purposes of the new reform agenda in which everyone was expected to achieve success. The answer: a new kind of test, one that could be directly taught to, didn't require as much secrecy regarding content, and above all no longer required scores that distributed students evenly along a predetermined curve. Everyone is urged to pass these new tests—although rank ordering and percentile scores are still used. These tests are intended to show whether teachers and kids are doing their prescribed jobs: teachers teaching to the test and students learning what's on them. It's called curriculum and test alignment. A number of states developed variants of this new sort of test, the Massachusetts Comprehensive Assessment System (MCAS) tests, the Regents in New York, the Texas Academic Assessment System (TAAS), and the Standards of Learning (SOL) in Virginia to name a few.

From the viewpoint of the test taker, these are very similar to the old tests, although generally they are much longer. From the viewpoint of the teacher, the big difference is that these tests can be openly taught to. From the viewpoint of the state, the scores are set not by test makers but by political officials in state departments of education. One might describe them as politically rather than technically normed tests. (For example, the weighting of subsections—how much each counts—and thus the actual scores, as well as the cutoff scores—what constitutes failure, what needs improvement, what is proficient—are in many states not decided until after the results are in and state officials can estimate the impact of their decisions; but in all states pretests give a pretty accurate estimate.) The meaning of a score on these new tests rests not with the neutral bell curve but with judgments made by some politically appointed body—ideally in collaboration with educational experts.

The new tests are more like the ones teachers or academic departments have long been accustomed to giving at term's end—covering what they think were the key elements of their courses. When they are the ones to set the scores, teachers too are influenced by political factors—who will blame them if the scores are too low, will they be believed if they are too high, what's the school's attitude toward marking on a curve? The technology is not necessarily dissimilar—teachers often use multiple-choice exams, for example. But unlike the designers of the new state tests, classroom teachers and local administrators are folks close to the action, "interested parties" in a position to modify their exams and scores based on their best judgment and aware of what actually is happening in their classrooms and schools. Of course, their very closeness is the reason why teachers are, in today's climate, distrusted.

How different are these new tests to design than the traditional norm-referenced tests? Largely the answer is, not a lot—except that the absence of the much-maligned bell curve complicates deciding what items to include and how to set expectations, scores, and cutoffs. Creating them begins the same way as any standardized test, with hundreds of teachers and expert academicians, under the direction of the (politically established) state education department, develop their wish lists of things they believe all students should know, appreciate, understand, and do at particular ages or grades; ideally these wish lists are tempered by experience. For example, one might wish all third graders could read the Harry Potter books; but is this goal reasonable? What about *To Kill a Mockingbird*? Shakespeare? Reading the California art standards for kindergarten, one is inclined to think that test makers had in mind the scope and sequence for a postdoctoral program in the arts. Could they possibly have had five-year-olds in their mind's eye when they wrote "students will research art genres (e.g., landscapes, seascapes, portraits), name an artist who worked in the genre, describe the artist's work, and then create an artwork that reflects the genre," or "students will talk about a work of art, telling what they think the artist is saying, and give reasons for their responses, using art terms (line color, shape)," or "compare and contrast a Renaissance landscape and a landscape by Richard Diebenkorn." (Actually, the latter came from the first grade standards.) In case you are curious, not only are similar requirements set for dance—"compare and contrast American square dances and English contra dancing," for example—but the same amazing expectations are repeated in every other subject discipline. California is not notably different from other states, nor are the arts standards any more humorous than those in history, math, literature, and science. When I sat on the New York State regent's advisory board, I ran across the following in health education for twelve-year-olds: students will demonstrate that they can cope with death and dying, as well as losing a friend. Why not?

Decisions regarding how to go from such pretentious wishes to actual items on a test are difficult, since they can't be based on how things would sort themselves out on a bell curve or any other predetermined ranking order (which would quickly cure test designers of such nonsense). In the absence of such a curve, decisions can be made that almost all children are appallingly lacking in artistic talent or coping skills and need earlier and more intensive remediation. Drill and practice in coping with death or identifying landscape genres?

However the decisions are made, the items will now produce a detailed scope and sequence of facts and skills deemed appropriate to directly teach to from kindergarten through twelfth grade. From now on the field is level, so proponents would argue: everyone knows what it is that might be on the test. Vague goals like "weighs evidence" or "writes with style" are hard to score objectively—and harder to teach to. Thus they are eliminated. The lists are often long. One esteemed educational laboratory figured out that covering all of the average state list would take nine more years of schooling. But no one wants their favorite items eliminated from the curriculum, since it is probable that only the stuff that makes it onto the test will ever be taught at all.

It is important to note that because the idea in many states is to at least appear more and more demanding, there is no obvious way to agree upon the reference base, as there is on traditional norm-based standardized tests. "But kids that age can't do that" and "teachers can't cover all that" may meet the response "but they should." This apparent nuisance, I will argue, is more than that: it is at the heart of why these tests cannot deliver what they promise. There are also some knotty content decisions that make such tests sink or swim politically. How (and whether) to teach about evolution, the Civil War, the labor movement, Reagan's place in history, the cause of World War I, or—as the state of Virginia (as I write this) is now finding out—what to say about the role of the Turks in the Armenian genocide, and whether to call it genocide. Decisions on these issues must now be made at the highest levels, and they must be given teeth so that they can be enforced in the form of tests. In fact, although it's easiest to see such controversies in the fields of social science and history, they abound in math and science as well as literature. (California's efforts to implement such a test were derailed a decade ago by the choice of certain multicultural texts as well as writing assignments that asked kids to write about personal experiences, and both California and Massachusetts are embroiled in wars over what math one should know and when.) The study conducted by the prestigious national educational laboratory (McREL) in Colorado, referred to above, points to the heart of the problem. There's simply no way in reality to cover all the content most states have deemed essential at any age, much less for graduation, assuming a child was supposed to learn this material mostly in school. Of course in real life, good sense takes over, and schools actually prepare kids only for a sufficient amount of the material that they discover, over time, is actually likely to be on the tests, and only that necessary to get a passing score, or to ensure that their schools look good compared with the competition.

The critical decisions involve the actual selection of which items from that long list to include on a particular test, as well as the wording of the questions and their possible alternate answers. Not everything in the curriculum framework can make it into one test! What kind of "distracters"—alternate wrong answers—should be included and how to decide? Posed one way the question will be an easy item; posed another, it will be hard. For example, "Was Lincoln the first or sixteenth president?" is easy and important to know. "Was Lincoln the thirteenth or sixteenth president of the United States?" is hard and is arguably not important to know. But both items may be used to enforce a standard that asserts that students should know when Lincoln was president. For this part of the work, the process is much the same as it was for the old standardized tests, involving both sample pretesting and statistical analysis—but again with a difference. For the old tests, the deciding factor was whether the scores produced were sufficiently and appropriately spread out; now that is not necessary.

After the pretesting, another difference between these new tests and traditional psychometric tests emerges. Since there's no need to tweak results to fit a rank ordered curve, the issue now is simply what to call the scores. When the first student took the newly minted MCAS, the Massachusetts Department of Education was free to decide that 80 percent of all students would be labeled less than proficient and fail the test as readers, and that zero percent demonstrated advanced status as writers. Since Massachusetts ranks high in language arts on all nationally normed tests, including the SAT and the National Assessment of Educational Progress (NAEP), the Department of Education's annual voluntary nationwide test of school skills, the decision may have seemed odd. In fact, the ensuing storm caused the department to lower the bar—amid protests that this was dumbing the test down—so that only 80 percent of urban kids would fail. As opposition increased, by the fourth year the department fielded a test in which fewer than half of all urban kids failed.

One celebrates and weeps simultaneously at the enormous distraction involved, the time and energy placed on the wrong goals.

Given the above oddity, it's not surprising that a test advertised to test "standards" becomes whatever is needed: a minimum competency test in some states (as in Texas and North Carolina), or "tough" (as in Massachusetts, Virginia, and New York, although now a student can eventually pass the MCAS with just 33 percent of the answers right on tests designed to measure math standards). Richard Rothstein reports in the *New York Times* that in the spring of 2000 in Ohio, 98 percent passed their high school graduation test, whereas less than half passed in California. And even fewer would have passed if the state had stuck with the educators' recommendations rather than those of the state commissioner, Delaine Eastin. Anomalies abound: only 28 percent of eighth graders were scored as proficient on the Massachusetts science exam, although their scores on international tests show them outranking every nation except Singapore. Conversely, North Carolina's state test showed 68 percent proficient in math, whereas only 20 percent were proficient based on a national science exam. The NAEP does not fare much better. Only 2 percent of high school seniors were labeled advanced on the federal Department of Education test of math, but twice that number alone pass advanced placement exams in math and 10 percent score above six hundred on the math SATs. Who is right? Who is wrong? These absurdities result from trying to adapt a technology never designed for such purposes.

In addition, such tests face a whole host of related conundrums that stem from the central fact that they have no basic reference point except political judgment. Equating tests—a technical term for comparing scores on tests that differ from year to year—is another once minor headache that these tests compound. Massachusetts, for example, has, to its credit, decided to make most items public each year; in other states the frameworks have changed frequently. In either case, new tests are needed. So is a score of seventy-two on one test the same, higher, or lower than a score of sixty-eight a year later on a new test? Discussing test rescoring in Texas, psychometrician Daniel Koretz, in *Education Week,* acknowledged that equating posed serious problems in the context of standards-based testing. Texas officials claimed that their 2001 test was harder than their 2000 test, that lower raw scores didn't mean lower performance—so they had added credit. The Massachusetts fourth grade English test was made easier the third year in response to complaints that the reading passages were almost all on a sixth through tenth grade difficulty level. When challenged regarding how scores should be compared from the second to third year, the Department of Education reassured the public that while the questions were easier, students now needed more right answers to get the same score. A similar problem arose in New York City when sixth grade scores were unaccountably much higher one year, owing, the test makers said (and New York City officials denied), to equating, with substantial consequences for promotional policies.

What is thus strikingly different about these new variants is not the tests themselves but the chutzpah of those who design and use them for high-stakes purposes despite these unresolved issues. The old test designers, who expected their tests to last a decade or longer, frankly claimed that teaching to them was unfair and invalidated the meaning of the scores, and that the items hadn't been selected for that purpose. The careful and fairly modest claims for when and how the tests should be used and the high measurement error involved in any single score stand in stark contrast to current claims for these new less rigorously designed tests.

The biggest differences between the old and new state-designed tests is that the new tests are put together much faster, require less technical validation and fewer reliability checks, are much longer, include more detailed factual questions, and are used for more high-stakes purposes. Also, the scores are no longer a mere artifact of the bell curve but are instead a mere artifact of the judgment of state commissioners. Each of these changes ought to be controversial. Yet they rarely are. For example, makers of the traditional psychometric tests claimed that tests for elementary school pupils were actually less reliable if they lasted too long—the score would be influenced by sheer exhaustion. An hour was viewed as the limit of technical reliability for children under ten. But tests that do not meet such criteria are routine for children who are seven and eight years of age these days. Test makers used to insist that the degree of measurement error (which was routinely made available to schools) precluded using scores for any high-stakes decisions. A score of 4.5 on a test did not mean the student was reading like a fourth grader in the fifth month of the year (which is how the numbers are translated), but in all likelihood the true score was somewhere between 3.9 and 4.9, and possibly higher or lower. Yet diplomas now hang on a much finer line of demarcation. Psychometricians haven't changed their mind, but their tests are now used to do what they formerly claimed was undoable.

The test makers agree that cities and states often use and abuse their tests. They themselves make modest claims, if asked, for what a test can tell us about individuals or schools. For example, "I am led to conclude," says Robert Linn, perhaps the preeminent leader in the field, "that the unintended negative effects of high-stakes accountability uses often outweigh the intended positive effects." But such claims carry little political clout, if they are noticed at all. The technical manuals, with their careful disclaimers, that accompanied such tests when I began teaching are no longer seen by school people.

The Impact on Schooling

While this new breed of tests is remarkably similar to the old one, we are no longer warned against teaching to the test. State officials in fact demand that we do so. The same publishers who make many of these new tests now publish coaching materials for their tests. If something is not likely to be on the test, the official word is, don't teach it. School officials in some states even argue that children's regular classroom grades should not be substantially different from their state test score grades. In Boston this wisdom was the basis of an explicit directive from the superintendent's office to all school personnel. Thus test scores and class grades do not become two different ways to measure progress but two ways to record the same test scores!

Because the tests now claim to measure exactly what should be taught, it is far easier (for better or worse) to script teaching down to a lesson for every day in the year, each corresponding to a set of potential test questions. Some districts mandate scripted lessons only for low-performing schools. This system makes it easier to standardize the textbooks used (ones that conform to the state's frameworks) and the preparatory material to order (testing companies now have both hard copy and on-line material for virtually every state test). And it simplifies as well the designing of teacher training.

Adopting such a system means that many a curriculum related to children's interests or contemporary or spontaneous events (a hurricane that just swept through town, the river that runs through the school's backyard, the coming to town of a great exhibit on the ancient Celts, the release of a great movie on World War II, or the attack on the World Trade Center) must be ignored—or at best noted only in passing—in order to cover the standardized test-driven fare. It's hard to justify spending whole months on any topic, much less one that might involve only one or two questions on the test—like ancient China or the Holocaust. The 1999 MCAS test, for example, includes one item on China—which requires knowledge about the thirteenth-century Song Dynasty—and none on the Holocaust. Furthermore, unless tests are devised for all subject areas, everything not being tested—like music, dance, the visual arts—is driven out of the curriculum.

The Old Disguised as the New!

The majority of the states who have jumped on this new bandwagon still use the same standardized norm-referenced tests described in chapter 6—but for this new and different purpose. Obviously impossible? State officials claim that it's reasonable to expect all students to be in the top half of the curve (or wherever the marker is set), even though, if the test makers don't abandon their psychometric reputations entirely, that will lead only to a raising of the grade level

cutoff score sometime in the future. Oklahoma now has a law speci-
fying that 90 percent of its students in third grade should be on grade
level on a currently normed test by 2007. If the superintendent is
lucky, that is sufficiently far in the future so that he or she will have
moved on to another job somewhere else by then. Paul Vallas in Chicago left his job because he was still around when the sad news was
announced that the high school scores were either unaffected by his
reforms or actually going down, while the elementary scores—on a
norm-referenced test used year after year after year—had gone up.
(In fact, however, he went out claiming victory.) Both Oklahoma and
Chicago are still using old-fashioned normed tests—with a twist.

The makers of the old normed tests have renamed their percentile
scores into four levels, called advanced, proficient, needs improvement, and failed. But how they did this is unexplained. For example,
on the norm-referenced Stanford 9 test, a student has to be in the
forty-ninth percentile to get a level two (i.e., to pass) the fourth grade
math test, whereas being in the twenty-second percentile is required
in language arts. These new names, labeled I–IV, have become the
language of the standards movement and thus are commonly used on
norm-referenced tests too. They were borrowed from the NAEP, the
granddaddy of standards-based tests. The NAEP was designed by
the U.S. Department of Education (DOE) to gather longitudinal data
based on small population samples. The NAEP's invention of the four
levels of proficiency, which is less than a decade old, is based strictly
on judgment calls by a panel of DOE-chosen experts with a reform
agenda. The names and labels are whatever test makers—including
the publishers of the Stanford 9 used in California or the Iowa Test of
Basic Skills used in Chicago and their respective state authorities—
choose to say they mean. Is there something Alice in Wonderlandish
about this?

Impact on Students

In the meantime, these tests lead to real-world consequences, for
a generation of youngsters, above all those already most vulnerable,

hang in the balance. While critics claim that the high school diploma has become worthless, it continues to have a very exact monetary value—as we have been reminding children for years in all our "stay in school" advertising campaigns. The dollar cost of adopting these new graduation requirements will fall heavily upon communities of color. To deny increasing numbers of students a high school diploma will also mean that large numbers won't be able to enter our two- and four-year colleges, at an even greater economic loss to the students, their families, and their communities. Whereas 70 percent of the seniors at Boston's famous Fenway High School failed the MCAS in 2000, before the high stakes went into effect 90 percent went on, as they have for years, to college and did well there. Students at over thirty famous small New York City high schools—like Central Park East Secondary School—which have been sending 90 percent of their students on to successful college careers, are similarly endangered— unless those schools drop the very practices that produced such past success to focus on the test. Test-mandated holdover policies have similar chilling effects. Every time we hold a child over, we are substantially reducing the odds of that child graduating anytime in the future—and once we hold a child over twice, the odds go down to less than 1 percent. Even before the standards movement attacked so-called social promotion, half the young black men in America were at least one year over age when they reached eighth grade. What happens now?

The first and foremost impact of the new standardization is already evident in the increased dropout rate in state after state. In a detailed study of the "Texas miracle," Boston University psychometrician Walt Haney documents how the very youngsters we just recently wooed into staying in school are now pushed out via tests. He notes that Texas continues to have the highest dropout rate in the nation. And dropout rates disguise the even larger number of students who "disappear" between sixth grade and twelfth grade. Many supporters acknowledge the increased dropout rates but claim they represent a passing phase, the necessary price to be paid until the system and the kids adjusts. The leaders of the testing drive in Massachusetts are asking folks to wait and see. Headlines in the *Boston Globe* assert that without pain there cannot be gain. These youngsters are, says the *Globe,* merely the necessary casualties of the war on behalf of high standards.

A state official in Massachusetts reassured legislators by noting that a student could get just 40 percent of the answers right and still pass. If one is measuring something important, getting 60 percent wrong is absurd. If one is measuring absurd things, however, it's another matter. It may be that the implicit denigration of the common-sense human judgment of the adults in kids' lives will be, in the long term, the greatest price paid in our current mania for high-stakes testing.

The Alternative to Standardization

The alternative to standardization is real standards. Standards in their genuine sense have always depended on the exercise of that suspicious quality of mind—our fallible judgment—and training ourselves, as Jefferson recommended, to the better exercise of such judgment.

The best doctors know the danger of tests that replace medical judgment. No diagnostic test stands by itself. And no diagnosis, no matter how uncontroversial, determines a good treatment plan. Treatment plans designed by HMO clerks or, for that matter, HMO doctors, far removed from patients, with access only to medical descriptions of patients' symptoms and copies of their test scores are not what patients need. They need doctors, with good medical training and good collegial and lay oversight, professionals accustomed to reviewing all the evidence. We are about to learn the same lessons in education.

To evaluate our local schools, we can collect evidence of various kinds in multiple forms, and we can bring in a range of external opinions—expert and lay—regarding the schools' reliability and validity. Debate, both local and national, is vital to the evaluation process. What we have to keep in the forefront is that data rarely speak for themselves. We must raise questions like "What evidence is there that this is or isn't an important trend?" and "What do we know about how this plays out and what interventions work best?" Second opinions must always be welcome. This kind of questioning is, after all, how we make judgments in most fields, including how we give doctoral candidates their PhDs. It's how judges vote on movies, books, and Olympic gymnasts. It's even how we decide matters of life and death in our jury system. The jury handbook I received last year bragged about the fact that untrained ordinary citizens were entrusted to carefully weigh important matters. Only the most egregious self-interests are ruled out.

If we want to find out what teachers and parents can do to help a particular child's reading, we will have to seek to understand how that particular child is tackling reading tasks. Both traditional test scores and the relatively short interview we use at Mission Hill may be inadequate. We may need to obtain second and third opinions. No shame need be attached to the fact that we have only the most imprecise tools for making these kinds of assessments, and that some are embedded in our daily interactions with the child and our close observation of the child at work in authentic settings. Two diagnosticians, be they teachers or doctors, may well disagree—even given the same set of X rays—but it helps if they have other real-life symptoms to check their theories out on. The tasks of measuring and interpreting what is going on in a child's head call for trained judgment—our knowledge of what to listen for and how to recognize the array of misunderstandings that might lie behind a child's errors. But these are one-on-one tasks, and they are time-consuming. Good listening can be informed by science, although in the end it remains an art. The art of good teaching begins when we can answer the questions our students are really trying to ask us, if only they knew how to do so.

For those occasional gatekeeping purposes—quite a different matter—we can develop systems such as those described elsewhere that have been used at hundreds of middle schools and high schools over the past few decades (but which are also being challenged now by the imposition of high-stakes standardized tests) for deciding when a child is ready to move on to the next level of schooling. We have a history that demonstrates how such local performance-based systems work, and even legislative proposals in various states to make these systems state policy. The systems vary; mostly they require schools and school districts to put together their own collection of standards, with a few spare common statewide indicators or tests.

All of these combine careful expertise, public evidence, and eventual reliance on human judgment, not hidden behind tests but right out front. The doctor must explain why she is recommending one form of treatment or another and what the trade-offs and side effects may be. She has to convince her patients, explain her reasoning, and discuss risks, not hide behind data as though the data spoke for themselves. Another doctor might disagree, might read the same sonogram or blood test differently based on other available evidence. Some patients might choose to change doctors. The same is true for educators. People often tell me that tests are part of real life, that kids need to be taught how to handle them. There's truth to this, and training in test taking is essential. But actually, far more often decisions are made by such real-life judges in a format closer to the one we use at Mission Hill for portfolio reviews.

At Central Park East Secondary School, we used to combine our in-house judgments—our standards—with a wide range of external reviews, including each year bringing a group of experts in one of the domains our students were required to pass muster on, to assess our assessments. The experts' task was critiquing us—the faculty—in an open and public forum. Their power was enormous, although there were no official sanctions attached to their findings.

The Price Paid

What worries me most is that in the name of objectivity and science—two worthy ideas—the testing enterprise has led teachers and parents to distrust their ability to see and observe their own children. In fact, objectivity and science start with such observation.

When parents and teachers no longer believe they can directly judge a child's reading ability, when they see the indirect evidence of tests as more credible, I fear for the relationships between children and the adults they must depend on to grow up well. I imagine what would have happened to my son had I not been ornery and in the habit of reading with him. I worry too when kids can't tell us whether they are good readers until they see their scores. I know then that one of the goals of a good education has been lost—"know thyself." Cornel West says that Malcolm X added to this: "to know thyself is painful." There are times that the *Globe*'s motto—"no gain without pain"—may apply; real self-knowledge is sometimes hard to come by. But avoiding it is not a solution.

We educators are paying the same price as we anxiously wait each year for our test scores to be reported. We now depend on such scores to assess our own kids and our own work. The staggering jump in "achievement" of Massachusetts high school students between 2000 and 2001, for example, wasn't noticed by any of the system's teachers, students, or principals until the day the scores were released to the press.

Imagine the effect on a parent of a third grader, beaming with pleasure at her son's apparent reading ability, when she discovers in a letter sent her by the state that he really can't read. Imagine the reverse as well. The withering away of the expectation that human beings can and must make judgments, even on matters so intimate and close to home, has frightful side effects. And for the young, to be adrift in a world in which those who know them best are told they do not know them at all undermines what growing up most requires: faith in adults and respect for their expertise. For a teacher who sees a kid day in and day out to admit that she won't know how well he reads until the test score arrives is not good news. (And once we are convinced of the magic of test scores, how easy it is, by the mere act of setting "cut scores" wherever we wish, to convince the public at large that this or that percentage of children are or aren't doing well—depending on our purposes and agendas.)

Creating a culture in which all kids use their minds powerfully is well within our reach. Resorting to flawed standardized testing, whose only virtue seems to be its capacity to enable us to pretend we can rank everyone (or sort everyone) precisely and objectively, is both unnecessary and counterproductive to such ends. The development of a theory and practice of assessment consistent with the democratic demand for high achievement for all children is not impossible, and some of the ingredients for such a new approach already exist. What I hope I have demonstrated is that the current wave of standards-based tests are not the answer.

At best, tests can take our temperature—sample where we're at and hazard an educated guess at what a rise or fall in temperature might mean. Tests are thermometers, not cures. Science simply won't solve these issues for us. As the old song goes, "We'll have to do it by ourselves." What we need are assessments—with low or high stakes —that place authority in the hands of people who actually know the kids, and make sure that the community, the family, and the student have ways to challenge such judgments—ask questions, present competing forms of evidence, check them out with a second opinion. We may find that old-fashioned standardized tests are one tool among many that will prove useful. We need, in short, standards in terms of both means and ends, not standardization.

CHAPTER EIGHT

The Achievement Gap

People of color, above all within the African American and Latino communities, face a special dilemma when it comes to the debate about standards and get-tough measures on schools. So much of the debate, across political lines, is about children of color, even when it is not explicitly so. And behind the debates, behind the impetus for tests and test-driven standards on the part of many, is the hope that finally there will be a solution to what is known as the achievement gap—the gap in achievement on almost all standard measures based on socio-economic class and income, and also the gap that is evident when race is viewed as a separate category.

The apparent achievement gap, as measured at least in terms of test scores, based on color and holding income and years of parental schooling constant, is shocking and significant. That's important to keep in mind. But it is also important to state right up front that the gap is not nearly as significant as it appears when income is ignored —and it usually is, when the statistics are presented to the lay public. And the gap would be even less so if we took into account real wealth—not just annual income—and accumulated family assets, both financial and social. The gap between social classes is today somehow a somewhat more comfortable one for many Americans to accept than the gap between races, and there is no organized constituency to demand that it be closed as well. So the economic gap is rarely regarded as a serious concern for reformers and politicians. As essayist Richard Rodriguez noted in an interview with Elizabeth Farnsworth on the *Lehrer News Hour,* members of America's middle class are more comfortable "sneering" at ignorance and failure when they are rooted in "trailer park trash" than when they originate in ghettos. Mike Rose's writing provides an eloquent reminder of how class plays itself out educationally.

But all that said, race remains a crucial category. The gap in measurable test data—and more important perhaps in dropout rates, graduation rates, college attendance, and graduation from college—remains after we correct for income and years of parental education (the only measure we have of class). When we look at the landscape of American political and social life, no issue stands out more critically, and of course it has been central to the work I've been immersed in. Until almost yesterday, the idea that the differences in achievement were due to racial disparities in intelligence was taken for granted by most whites; such differences therefore required no explanation. Even a mere twenty years ago, in a book (*The Bell Curve*) that made the best-seller list and was talked about everywhere, Richard Herrnstein and Charles Murray concluded that they had proof that the centuries-old canards about low black intelligence was a fact, sad but true. That does not mean, they said, that black Americans don't deserve fair treatment, but this understanding should inform social policy. Conservatives rallied to the authors' defense when they were accused of racism. Don't blame the messenger if the message bothers you, supporters argued. On the basis of reams of IQ data—much like the current reams of achievement data—Herrnstein and Murray claimed to demonstrate that the gap between whites and blacks, on average, was profound and could not be explained by any factor other than race alone. Liberals argued back that racism had taken a toll on black communities and that where differences exist they result from environmental factors rather than biological ones. Some noted correctly that IQ was an artifact that was sensitive not to basic genetic and biological differences but to cultural differences—the worlds that blacks and whites lived in that led them to respond to certain phenomena in different ways, including test items. What these studies picked up on was how profound an impact racism has had on our society—not how inferior blacks were or how superior whites were, but how unnaturally different they had become, at least if one looked at them only through the lens that such tests focused on. The literature critiquing IQ tests was summoned forth correctly (though not radically enough, I'd argue) in defense of black intellect.

But damage was done—for it reinforced a prejudice so deep, so fearful, and so great, and societally so pervasive, that it would take more than logic to dislodge it. And every black person—perhaps above all, middle-class blacks—labored under that raging fear. No sooner did the IQ tests fade into the background than new evidence was discovered. Test scores on other dimensions (aside from IQ) seemed to confirm these fears and prejudices. Whether schools were run by blacks or whites, no matter how much additional money was spent, regardless of class sizes or changes in textbooks or pedagogies—the gap between white and black achievement (holding data on socioeconomic status aside) remained deep. Many sadly noted that only artificial measures (affirmative action) provided any opportunity for the children of color who appeared brightest and most academically successful to get into college, where they often flourished, or to move into job situations where in reality they were able to handle the demands of the workplace. But affirmative action came with a price and could not long be counted on. But "objectively"—on scientifically designed measures of competence, not subjective performance-based measures—whites always (on average) outperformed blacks. And the more strenuously efforts were made to undercut racism and the more effort was poured into improving test scores, the more obvious was the test score achievement gap between whites and blacks. As scores of black students rose, those of white students rose even faster.

One eminently reasonable response from African Americans was that the problem was race all right, but not the racial inadequacies of their children. The problem was the racism of teachers—overwhelming white—in our schools. They were either intentionally or unintentionally miseducating children of color. "Institutional racism" is the useful shorthand term for describing the myriad of ways in which the school experiences of children of color were injurious to their achievement. It was time to fix the schools—and fast. Every day the pattern continued it poisoned the spirits of more black children and supported the biases of their oppressors.

The easiest answers lay in the inferior resources generally provided to schools that served most black kids, or the portions of white schools where black kids more often found themselves consigned. But the sociologists of education soon compiled data purportedly proving that the gap remained even when schools equalized funds. (Of course, the only data that counted were test scores.) The gap persisted even when black kids attended schools and classes that predominantly served white kids and thus supposedly got exactly the same services. Then, said black educators, the problem must be subtler than we thought. There is something in the ideological assumptions in schools—whether they be progressive or conservative—that undermines our kids; something in the subjective mind-set of teachers that carries with it damaging messages to black kids. From the moment they enter schools they meet a relentless but quiet form of racism that says in one way or another—you're not as good, you're unable to, you can't. Some may say it with kindness and apparent affection; others directly. Who knows which is worse? The message may even come from black teachers imbued with the values and assumptions of a white-dominated system and system of thinking.

This was and is a powerful indictment, and it is hard to disagree with. I don't. It was resisted by conservatives and most liberals for many years. But I saw plenty of evidence for it in my experience in schools, including some of my own.

When I began teaching thirty-five years ago, these issues were already on the table. Fierce disputes raged as to whether "disadvantaged" children (above all, poor black and Hispanic children) came to school without language. Schools were filled with teachers who held such beliefs, buttressed by studies that suggested they were right. Not only did these children lack grammar and vocabulary, not to mention the ability to articulate sounds properly, but also the words they did know were valueless, the research said to teachers, for building high levels of achievement. Furthermore, research showed that these children had very limited experiences, above all the type of experiences upon which one might be able to build a decent education. Although there were critics who charged the research was nonsense, or distorted, such was the fashionable view of most established educational institutions, held even by the reformers of the sixties. And it's a view that still holds enormous influence in decisions about curriculum, reading material, and pedagogic strategies for filling in the missing pieces that differentiate white middle-class and black children (class distinctions are often not made). It's a view I largely disagree with, and although it raises some legitimate points—some kids do have severely limited worldly experiences, for example, and poverty does take a toll in young children's cognitive development—it has at least as much relevance to the educational difficulties of poor white as poor black kids, and almost nothing to do with middle-class blacks.

When I came to Philadelphia in 1965 to teach in the first Head Start program in the country, the deficit model ideology about poor children—above all, poor black children—dominated the teacher training we received and the recommendations about what the children needed to be taught. Both black and white leaders echoed it. We were to teach children the stuff their families had been too ignorant to teach them: like the names of the letters of the alphabet and their colors, and how to raise their hands and work cooperatively. Direct, explicit teaching was favored as being better suited to disadvantaged children from nonmainstream cultures. In addition, they needed more exposure to books and high culture—trips to the zoo were seen as culturally important. And above all, we were to teach to the tests—mostly IQ tests at first—so that scores would go up.

In contrast, progressive educators, going back to arguments put forth a hundred years earlier by the founders of the kindergarten movement in Italy and Germany, argued instead for more play, on the assumption that this was valuable for all humans, but above all for lower-class children whose harsher life circumstances had deprived them of the kind of playful experiences from which conceptual and abstract thought derived, experiences that maximized the imaginary capacities that higher-level thinking rested on. They quoted Piaget and other more contemporary child developmentalists, and my own experiences confirmed these theories to some degree—although given the misunderstandings between school and family, they struck me as probably exaggerated. But I agreed with the progressives that the best way to improve test scores was to do for all children even more of what we already did for wealthy children—and that play was the vehicle for strong intellectual development in the young, regardless of class or race. What was good for the rich was best for the poor too—only more so.

Still others argued that nothing would matter—the argument was moot—until we got the relationship between schools, the children, and their families better aligned. Kids came to school with skills and talents we were not building on, they argued. Until the experiences of home and school were made more continuous and natural, and parents had reason to trust that their children were being sent to schools that respected them—we wouldn't get far with any but the most exceptional children. Children couldn't use schools well for serious learning until schools were more trusted. In Mike Rose's words, what was lacking was "an orientation toward the interaction of poverty and ability that . . . enables us to see simultaneously the constraints poverty places on the play of mind and the actual mind at play within those constraints." But what we understood less about were "the constraints" of being a racial minority that were placed on "minds at play."

I was, first and foremost, in that latter camp, that focused on repairing the gap between school and family—whether its source was racial or economic. Agenda item number one for folks like me was getting the relationships right, and agenda item number two was tackling the questions of curricula and pedagogy that divided progressives from conservatives. In real life, of course, the two items went hand in hand. For many of us, the key issue in terms of curriculum was re-

thinking the meaning of academics, which had been skewed historically in the interests of certain histories and stories rather than others:
why some subjects and some fields of study were considered high status and others were low, for example, the false dichotomy between the
practical and the "academic," and so on. Addressing issues of curriculum and pedagogy required examining assumptions about the objectivity of time-honored forms of rewarded intelligence, about how
we heard school language versus children's home language, about artificial school norms and other accepted and acceptable communal
norms.

Neither of these two agenda items could be addressed separately
from the other. Until we got the relationships righter, we'd make little
progress by tackling just the in-school factors. And neither could pro-
ceed very far without major system changes. The road would, at best,
be rocky, if we agreed to go down it at all. And in the absence of a larger
social push to tackle the racism and class inequities that permeate the
society families and children live in, successes would be limited even
when we could make a concerted effort to focus on our alternate reform agenda.

These theories were buttressed by what I experienced in school,
listening to kids on the playground, getting to know their families—
starting as early as 1964 at the largely African American school I taught
at and where my own children went to school. Kids who were silent in
class were noisy and talkative with their family and friends outside of
school. After a while, it was easy to believe Frank Smith's documented
claim that all children learn approximately ten new words a day—
regardless of class or race—although not necessarily the same words.
And clearly, given the opportunity, kids reveled in playing with language (and language play turns out to be a strength of many black children, a fact that shouldn't surprise us given other evidence of the his-
toric importance of storytelling and wordplay and verbal eloquence in
the black community).

Fascination with the world knew no class or race or ethnic bounds.
While all children were bored by the standard curriculum, none were
bored by studies of ancient Egypt or dinosaurs—despite their irrele-

vance, and all enjoyed learning about batteries and bulbs, sink and
float, and other neat science experiments. Of course, much depends
on which differences you focus on (and whether you lump all black
kids together and begin to see and hear what you've already decided is
there). When I was teaching little kids to read in central Harlem, I realized that kids were expected to recognize homonyms, homophones,
and rhyming words even if they didn't match the kids' own dialects.
For example, for some kids *pin* and *pen* made the same sound, although they had different meanings and different spellings. I didn't
get it right away, but these differences made some teachers see such
kids as hearing-impaired or not paying attention or inattentive to
sounds. These teachers recommended special ed classes for these kids.

There are children who arrive in school unsure of what the routines are for being good and bad, and thus they retreat into being over-
cautious and withdrawn or bad and naughty. Many are boys whose
ways of getting attention and praise at home bring nothing but cen-
sure at school, so they settle for badness as the best of a bad bargain
(a phenomenon that affects boys across racial lines). These children
were more often recommended to special ed classes too. Some pioneering sociologists took the trouble to listen to kids outside of school
and concluded that "deprived" families spoke as much to their kids as
did anyone else—although the particular patterns of speech and vocabulary might differ. Even the most loving teacher sends messages
about how she sees your family and your lifestyle, messages that lead
some sensitive little children not to share too much out of family loyalty. Schools tell kids what they value and treasure, and what it is they
don't, in ways they do and don't intend. There are signs in the way we
greet kids, what songs we sing, how we decorate our walls that say "this
land belongs to you"—but not to me. I learn every day.

My liberal sentiments were confirmed by reality—just as reality also
unsettled me. But I assumed that if we sent different messages, had
different relationships with families, and reshaped the curriculum
and pedagogy, the outcomes would be substantially different—even if
gaps remained. With a group of similarly minded colleagues, we fol-

lowed a cohort group of ordinary kids at Public School 144 in central Harlem from prekindergarten through second grade. We felt confident that we were making a difference and that their reading test scores would show the world how much good schooling could accomplish. We gloated. Instead, they did more or less as badly as all other children from the neighborhood on the second grade citywide test of reading. As I described in chapter 6, they seemed confidently wrongheaded in giving the answers to questions that white kids I knew breezed through correctly, including far less-skilled white kids—even when they read the passages with confident fluency. Who was wrong? Me or the tests? And how was I to explain the discrepancy to the parents who had perhaps trusted me?

What was clear was that it was not easy to be convincing, even to the parents whose children we taught. The tests confirmed their worst fears, and although some trusted us enough to hold on to their confidence in their children based on direct knowledge, others were shaken. A substantial number, even if not a majority, came to the conclusion that a white-controlled system was, intentionally or not, depriving their kids of needed skills and information, stuff they wouldn't do if the kids were white. Parents said it loud and clear at meetings I attended during the 1967 and 1968 teacher strikes. Among my black colleagues, there was a larger and subtler sense of unease about the prejudices they felt the system and their white colleagues harbored and its impact on "their kids." But for both conservative and traditionalist white educators, the discrepancies the tests showed between black and white kids were simply the facts of life. No surprise.

Today, on the other hand, as income disparities soar, these same conservatives and traditionalists are surprised, insisting that neither race nor class should have any impact on academic achievement, that all that earlier stuff about biological differences was either untrue or irrelevant, and that if differences appear it's the fault of public schools, or ineffective teachers, or both. The issue is not bad genes or low IQs anymore. Nor is it poverty. Rejoice. Even the Left and Center have abandoned explanations based on race and class. "Of all the facts we study—class size, ethnicity, location, poverty—they all pale to trivial-ity in the face of teacher effectiveness," says statistician William Sanders, as quoted in the conservative Heritage Foundations magazine. Others tack on bad attitudes on the part of too many parents who excuse their children's poor school performance—recycling that sixties concept of "the culture of poverty."

I find myself oddly unnerved by this new consensus. It seems obvious that poverty, as well as racism and subtler class injuries, are partly to blame for differences in educational outcomes, even outcomes I accept as important, not merely test scores. Surely the fact that some schools are less well funded matters. Surely, as a parent, I used my advantages to give my kids advantages. The new official consensus that you shouldn't blame society, inequality, money, racism, or poverty—those are mere excuses for a failure of parenting, schooling, and teaching—seems wrongheaded, but in a new way. True enough, excuses encourage laziness and fatalism on the part of students, which undermine their needed efforts to succeed. But is *excuses* the right word for such facts of life? Many black leaders, relieved to no longer be attacked as basically inferior, echo the "no excuses" sentiment in the hopes that it will build a bonfire under inept school systems that do not deliver for their kids. Maybe we can blast out teachers' subtle racism with fear of job loss or other sanctions, they argue. Maybe demanding higher test scores will do what workshops on race haven't. Isn't any bonfire better than none? While getting the society to eliminate racism and inequality on a larger scale seems temporarily, maybe making a dent on test scores is within reach, some liberal defenders of increased testing argue.

As a result, in the present climate, even the claim that maybe racism and poverty are factors that lead some kids to have less effective teachers and schools is seen by many as an excuse, which will in turn lead to lessening the pressure on kids, parents, and teachers to improve their work. If black kids, as a friend of mine recently reported with anguish, wince when they see endlessly proliferating headlines and graphs comparing blacks and whites, the hope seems to be that these comparisons will motivate, not discourage, them. The truth will make them free, or maybe it depends on how they interpret it. What is it we want them to make of the truth? "Provide me with the words to turn the sting into something useful!" pleads a black teacher in a big failing Boston high school over the Internet.

Given my experience, I was glad when the word went out that schools needed to have high expectations for all children, that no kids should be labeled uneducable and written off. We would discover that every kid is smart—if we could tap into their smartness and make it work for them. If we weren't succeeding with all kids, then it was schools that had to change—us, their teachers, our routines, our books, our ideas. And maybe we had to change dramatically if we were out to do a job that schools were not originally intended to do. Schools designed to sort—in ways that exaggerated racial and class differences— needed to be overhauled, from bottom to top, if they were to do quite the opposite. Just changing schools would not do it all, but I also believed that we had a chance to even the playing field substantially if we used schools properly.

I took it for granted that having a family of musicians would increase the odds that children would be talented at music and would have a greater chance at future success as musicians. It was hardly rocket science to see that this was true of almost all the special talents that families possess. And it was easy to see that this didn't require a biological or genetic explanation. Still, the right music lessons and lots of practice can surely help. And schools that told some kids to keep their mouths shut at singing time because they hadn't yet learned how to sing in tune were hardly likely to help—a practice quite common during my childhood. Schools that only recognized the musicality behind some kids' tastes, and put down other families' music, wouldn't help level the playing field either. In short, how we responded to those background differences was critical.

So that's where I started and where I still stand. But what about the gap between scores for kids who come from equally privileged families—except for the fact that one is white and the other black? How do I account for that, and will the kinds of changes I'm proposing for schools at large have a favorable impact on that gap?

And if they don't, are they worthy of the trust that I'm insisting is needed?

The answers I see lie elsewhere, in two messages that I hope have come through so far: (1) the tests aren't measuring what we think they are, and (2) as long as we focus our attention on that one gap, we won't focus on the gaps we might realistically make some progress with. Schools can make a difference, alter the gaps, in the real world success of kids—equalizing their power as citizens and wage earners. Tests underpredict actual achievement in life for women, African Americans, Latinos, and all low-income people, and they overpredict success for the wealthy and white and male. That's a fact, and one that further undermines children's chances at getting the kind of schooling that will matter. The white kids who got a combined SAT score of 1200 at my school weren't even in the same league intellectually as the African Americans who got 1000. I'm not talking about social or affective skills—just plain school academic smarts. Studies have shown over and over that this perception is a fact. Thus are advantages compounded. What we're trying to close are both real and phony gaps: the test score gap is one we've invented, and could uninvent. But until we nail it down, we will have a hard time insisting that we focus on the real gaps—which won't go away by themselves and which, even if we stopped testing kids, won't disappear until we tackle the reforms this book advocates, plus some that go beyond schooling. Here again are the reasons why the gap in test scores is the wrong focus:

1. Standardized tests, of almost all sorts, are peculiarly suited to enlarging class and race distinctions—to making the right answer seem more obvious to the "ins" than the "outs." As long as tests must rank students, it is naive to imagine they are going to rank on criteria that won't give the current "haves" advantages over "have nots"—it's even hard to do! If rich and poor experience life differently, blacks and whites do too. Standardized tests are, for this reason peculiarly suited to enlarging all sorts of differences. If I wanted to rank order my own three children, I could develop a psychometrically reliable and valid test to accomplish this—but why? What would doing this tell me?

2. Among the things standardized tests are sensitive to is class, but not just income and number of years of schooling one's parents had. They are also good at picking up on how many generations of class you have behind you—what your assets are, the old boys' networks you can call on. They are good at detecting not only how many years of college but also which college. This sensitivity, in turn, exaggerates race differences, since middle-class people of color are far more likely to be new to their wealth and status. In a recent interview, Lani Guinier, talking about the SAT, puts it this way: "William Julius Wilson and others have done studies showing that . . . the best predictor of your performance on these aptitude tests is your grandparents' socioeconomic status. These tests are a form of intergenerational wealth transfer."

3. And where test items don't discriminate by class and race, test designers seem to get nervous. As Jay Rosner noted in looking at the pool of items from which the SAT is drawn, or as I noted in looking at items that seven-year-olds face (see chapter 7), some items are, in a subtle way, more likely to be answered correctly by whites than blacks for no obvious reasons that suggest an intellectual difference. Test items that appear—on the surface, mind you—to be equally good discriminators of math or vocabulary skills and that show a "black preference" (meaning that blacks get them right more often) virtually never make it into the final test. Could it be otherwise? Yes. (It would perhaps also help if test makers and researchers made the extra effort to explore with real kids the reasoning behind their different responses to test questions.)

4. And once such tests are allowed to stand for achievement, they reinforce the very qualities of schooling that do the damage to start with. Kids who score poorly, whole communities of them, are given a less demanding education. They spend more time on remedial tasks, are taught in a more rote fashion, and are far more likely to be held over in grade, an experience that itself depresses their academic achievement and increases the gap in white and black graduation rates. But just as seriously, schools that focus on test smarts undermine the life smarts upon which intelligence builds—and over time

convince kids they haven't got what it takes. Tests become a cause of failure, not a mere documenter of it.

5. Some researchers (see Claude Steele's work published in *The Atlantic Monthly*) have demonstrated that black kids do worst on tests precisely when the stakes seem highest—above all when what's at stake is their own self-respect. When told that a test will measure their intelligence or academic competence, the most highly successful black young people do worse than when they are told that the test is just to help researchers understand how we all think. What's interfering is something Claude Steele labels "social distrust" when confronting a "stereotype threat." (Steele notes that the same principle is at work for any group that sees itself stereotyped as inferior in any particular trait or skill.)

6. High test scores, whatever they might predict, are unable to predict teamwork abilities, perseverance, risk taking, creativity, or old-fashioned reliability, not to mention any of the other hard skills that aren't being measured. So these qualities, which are essential in real life, become undervalued. Of course. So it's hardly surprising that at best the tests predict first-year college grades. And as Lani Guinier and Susan Sturm note in *Who's Qualified?*, a recent book on affirmative action, at worst they predict who is less, not more, likely to make a civic contribution to society.

7. And given how the tests work, they are the last indicator that is likely to change. If I want to close the gap between my three children, I'll have to value their differences, not their samenesses. I'll have to count the ways each of them has for being quite special. I'll have to observe closely so that I can increase their opportunities to make the best of their strengths and cope with their weaknesses. So rather than being rewarded for effort, kids and schools that aim to build on children's own drives and interests are as often as not penalized for doing so in a regime of schooling built around standardized test scores—of the new or old variant. Worst of all, schools built around short-term numerical goals threaten long-range goals in schools much as such a narrowed focus does in the world of business. The evidence suggests that harnessing student drives and interests is essential to making a long-term difference, even if it may have minimal impact on annual scores.

Furthermore, the focus on short-term test results also undermines practices associated with the development of a real work ethic, the conviction that perseverance will win out, as kids too often struggle helplessly to overcome their immediate testing handicaps and see less qualified peers outscore them. Finally, painfully, the more we focus on test scores, the more those with a testing advantage to start with will see their scores go up—thus widening the gap.

Together these factors suggest far different conclusions about the achievement gap. They suggest, in fact, that it may be something quite different after all.

A gap exists, and we can do much to make it smaller. But if I expect to make a difference in the real gaps, I'll have to invent different kinds of schools and different ways to hold them accountable for their work, ways consistent with the trust that needs to exist between learner and teacher, school and family. I'll have to choose the gaps I want to close first with care—and I'll pick those that count most and are also susceptible to change: getting a high school diploma for starters, followed by the capacity to do well as a college student, as an employee, as a citizen and neighbor and family member.

Test preparation—good coaching—helps in the short run. And since the winners are sure to be getting some pretty expensive coaching, where we can't get rid of the tests we need to be skillful at teaching all kids how to do their best with them—as long as doing so doesn't replace actually educating them. One can't avoid this distraction. If I'm going to administer a test to a student, she has a right to know how it works and how to make good guesses (at least by the time she reaches high school). I need also to think through the implications of Steele's analysis of the "stereotype threat" as it applies to preparing kids for all life's tests—what messages might be enhancing rather than undermining that threat. In short, however, while I won't ignore the paper-and-pencil type of standardized tests, I'll aim first and foremost at the tests of life.

And I do not underestimate the difficulties implied in insisting that we stick with a focus on more fundamental intellectual skills and habits. I just don't think there's a faster route. It's not patience but impatience that drives me on.

What the schools that make a demonstrable difference in the real achievement gaps in society do has a lot to do with establishing on a daily basis climates of social trust of the type that Claude Steele describes. I had a discussion once with some kids about the old television show called *All in the Family,* a spoof (so I thought) on racist working-class whites. Not a single one of the black or Latino adolescents in my class could even believe that I thought it was meant to be funny, was an attack on racism. They cited chapter and verse, and it was, I could quickly see, not an argument that rational discourse on commonly agreed-upon evidence was going to settle. We were, to this extent, seeing the world from different places. How could I be trusted to interpret the world for kids who saw it so differently than I did? Would I always know when and how to protect them from injuries that I didn't even recognize existed? Social trust is not easy to come by. But we can come a lot closer.

Some of the gaps we need to worry about require a direct political assault. These include the gap between the resources that are available to some kids and not others—including those that we've denied kids because we claim they don't affect their test scores! One gap to focus on is the quality of teacher expertise provided, which is a tougher task than imposing more tests, but one not made easier by our relentless bashing of the people who teach poor kids—not to mention their lower salaries and inferior working conditions. I'll believe money doesn't count the day that the rich stop spending so much on their own children.

But even if we got all these factors right, and we're a long way from doing so, we need also to fix the quality of relationships we have with kids and their families. Kids must see the grown-ups in their schools as belonging to the same universe as those at home, so that they can usefully keep company with them both. It won't be possible to tackle the subtler gap between races, language communities, and classes without building cultures of trust that overlap race, language, and class and that allow for all children and all families to feel they are respected members of a shared—and beloved—community.

PART THREE

A Broader Vision

CHAPTER NINE

Scaling Up: Stacking the Odds in Favor of the Best

Progress is not doing better what should not be done at all.
—Anonymous
If it's worth doing, it's worth doing poorly.
—Anonymous

Forty years ago, when I began working in Chicago, we were told that small, intimate, and personalized schools and strong school-family ties customary in the school of the privileged were not what "those kids" needed. I was told—bluntly—that the kinds of schools I attended in my privileged youth would not be good for most of the youngsters in Chicago's South Side. The style was appropriate for gifted children, for wealthy children, and maybe even for children with special needs, but not for ordinary children, and surely not for poor black children. It was a belief held almost as strongly by pro-claimed antiracists as by racists. It has gradually receded, though it is still heard behind the scenes or has reemerged in new language.

Thirty years of successful experiments have helped convince people that we can create public schools for all children more like what we have traditionally offered our very best and wealthiest students, and that when we do so, the results are better both academically and socially, above all for the children now failing. That's a step forward.

Today the detractors of small-school reform in public education mostly argue something different: that the kinds of experiments embodied in the stories of our schools can't translate into national, state, or even local policy—because they aren't "replicable." Valuable as such schooling can be, critics now argue, its successes are too idiosyncratic, requiring too many unusual people and unusual resources. Each year a few new ones flicker brightly in the limelight, and a few old ones die a natural death.

As a wise friend recently asked me, "Given the number of administrators and teachers who are not so good, and given the well-known political machinations of a lot of school boards, do your kind of schools have a prayer?" Building schools on the basis of trusting those closest to the action is the stuff of private education and cannot be imported into the public sphere on a large scale, even many of our staunchest supporters conclude. There aren't enough good people to go around. While the total number of exceptional schools that survive and thrive is substantial, it's insufficient to affect the vast majority of children who need a better education. Both conservative and liberal policy types agree that they cannot be the wave of the future.

For those of us who share the vision I have of schools, the challenge of "scaling up" is the most daunting one we face. It won't be easy, and it includes changing the way we think about both good schooling and systemwide school reform itself. But we know a great deal now about what kind of schools make a big difference, and we have some critical experiences that suggest what the next systemic steps might be, how such change could indeed be the "wave of the future."

Contrary to the mythology, exceptional schools do not die off, most are killed by intentional acts, not by the inevitable forces of nature. In nature, variation, "messiness," and chaos are not unnatural or unproductive forms of organization. In fact, as biologists would remind us, they are essential features of growth. When school people seek to forbid such messiness, or view it as a burden, we undermine the possibility of proliferation. Charismatic founders aren't easily replaced, but schools over time find alternate solutions if allowed to; good staff don't burn out as though they were appliances, but they do succumb to exhaustion if they must always straddle the fence between the old and the new. Times change, and schools must too—although change doesn't need to mean starting over from scratch whenever the district's political leadership shifts. Many good schools die an early unnatural death because the policies that govern our public systems cut short their natural growth. If we allow only the standardized models to pass inspection, we can't claim to be surprised that the others don't flourish!

This is a case where safety and longevity do not lie in numbers. Increased numbers create increased visibility, which in turn creates new demands to bring iconoclastic schools into compliance. Their mainstream counterparts ask why the mavericks are allowed to "get away" with this or that. Suspicions arise, and may even be encouraged, that their successes are due to being allowed to serve different kids, having larger per-pupil budgets, or otherwise engaging in practices that hurt the other schools. (In Boston, many teachers believed that the fiscal problems they were experiencing in the late nineties were due to the creation of ten small pilot schools, a belief fostered by some downtown budget folks.)

Then, finally, as they encounter new roadblocks, which require new Herculean responses, teachers begin to complain of weariness—the original fire in the belly that fueled the pioneering spirit begins to wane. They grow weary of always having to prove again that their approaches work, of never reaching a point where they can relax their warrior stance. As the leaders of the schools pass on into retirement, it becomes easier to replace them with folks who do not represent the viewpoint of the school community, who haven't the tenacious drive to keep working against the grain, or who are imposed in order to bring the schools into line.

The people who operate the present system do not see themselves in the business of trying to maintain idiosyncratic practice. As I discovered in my early efforts to produce some changes in a few schools in Manhattan's District Two, efforts to match teacher and school are even seen as absurd: "Why, Debby, what would happen if we began to worry about whether each teacher was in the right place?" Nor could they organize such matches if they wanted to—as this hapless bureaucrat who actually would have liked to please me demonstrated. They've been trained to seek, first and foremost, ways to solve problems by rule. If it's not good for everyone, it's not good for anyone. To make exceptions smacks of favoritism and inefficiency.

Of course, all school-based folks work hard at sabotaging this system; they spend their energies building special relationships with downtowners so that they can get away with nonconformity, break a rule here or there, be the recipient of special favors. They know that in fact schools can't be run, even poorly, the way the rules are written. But each exception must be defended, won over and over again. Each depends on energy devoted to caring for the system and its key players in an industry desperately short of energy for its central task. The problem is not malice, a clash of personalities, or egos, but ways of working built for different purposes.

The systems we have designed to manage schooling—even in small districts—follow a familiar recipe for unsuccessful organizations, be they public or private: they treat people as though they were interchangeable parts. One qualified teacher is seen as the same as another, one licensed principal right for any principal's slot. A principal recounted the state of anger and mourning on her staff when she was ordered to replace one writing program with another (the district had decided to drop the one it had been using, although it had won awards for the program over the years). The district also sent in a new math coach to help meet a districtwide allocation of personnel, replacing the one teachers had worked with for two years. The new writing program—with its new training component—was, teachers were assured, just as good as the old; ditto the new math coach. The current bureaucratic ideal is a machine, not a messy human invention— the bigger, more centralized and more rule-constrained, the better. For some schools the dysfunctional structures are of no great consequences— they serve kids who need only an occasional pat on the back to thrive competitively, get into the right colleges, get decent paying jobs, and so on. (Put aside the social and intellectual impact of bad schooling.) For other schools and other students, these structures spell disaster.

In fact, there is remarkable consensus about what the major features of good schools are, and they clearly don't match the bureaucratic model we've designed for public education. A consensus exists about the kinds of schools that work best, based not only on our extensive recent experience with alternative education, but also on what the rich have always known was good for their kids.

1. The schools that work best are small. Within them, people are not anonymous and interchangeable. Even in existing big schools, the kids that do best belong to small, intimate subschools with a strong culture of specialness. They hang out with "their teachers," "their clubs," and "their classmates." Feedback isn't bureaucratic, but direct and frequent, and everyone feels (and is) safer. It's harder not to know what's going on.

2. Schools that work best think of themselves as self-governing. They accept being held accountable for their work because they are in charge of making major workplace decisions. The details of their governance structures differ widely, and the balance between the immediate school and other larger interests, between teachers, parents, lay citizens, students, and alumni will vary as well. But every step away from these central actors—the people responsible for implementing policy—the weaker the translation between ends and means will be. (Besides, try getting kids to respect powerless people.)

3. Schools that work best are places of choice. They feel special to those who belong to them. It helps if there are sufficient choices available for parents, students, and teachers so that schools can afford to be different from one another—to have their own character, emphases, and style of operating that appeal to some but not to all. Good schools thrive on the eager and passionate loyalty of their members—past and present.

These three qualities—smallness, self-governance, and choice—offer a good beginning, and few parents when seeking a good workplace either for themselves or for their children wouldn't prefer one that met all three.

Critics say, yes, these are all good ideas, but they are utopian if we're talking about public education on a large scale. They constitute a prescription for individual schools that won't translate when we're talking about changing systems. The critics give several reasons why the ideas won't work, none of them convincing.

Critics say that the successes of small schools rely on too many one-of-a-kind phenomena—for example, the exceptional talents of the kind of people motivated enough to start them. Now, obviously, schools based on these principles work better with more talented staff members (and kids). But what leads us to think that untalented people perform better in settings that lack all three qualities? Or that they will do better in more impersonal settings? Furthermore, it's interesting to note that almost all the small schools in New York City have survived and thrived for more than twenty years with their second and even third generation of leadership. Under its third director, Jane Andrias, Central Park East is more exciting than it has ever been, and the CPE schools alone have nurtured at least a dozen school heads who now lead interesting small local schools or small school work, from teachers who would probably never have dreamed of being leaders of ordinary schools. Such schools don't depend on exceptional people (except, perhaps, to get them going in hostile political times); what they do best is create exceptional talent.

Critics also say that these schools work because they get special resources. First of all, that's typically untrue. Mission Hill, like all the Boston pilot schools, for instance, makes different choices about how to allocate the identical per capita budget allocated all schools in Boston. Why, however, are schools with scarcer resources less in need of smallness, self-governance, and choice? One might even argue that these three qualities become more important the scarcer the talent and the scarcer the resources, not the other way around.

Finally, critics argue that too many of these schools would make an impossible system to maintain: how would we keep track, hold schools accountable, report to the public if all schools were operating to a different drumbeat? But let's be honest. We surely don't do any of these well now; we have barely any credible data even for systems designed for uniformity, except for the charade of statistics coming out of tests, as I hope I've shown. So let's invent new solutions. Fortunately, there is a history of other successful possibilities consistent with what we know makes for good schools.

The success of the work of Anthony Alvarado in East Harlem and Stephen Phillips in the New York alternative high school division are important examples of what is possible for all children on a grand scale if we match good schools with good systems. Alvarado spent ten years slowly creating a districtwide system of choice that could survive his departure, and he used the lessons he learned there to redesign another district in the same city. In *Almost Home,* a book published twenty-five years after Alvarado began his work, David Kirp, public policy professor at the University of California, asserts that District 4 remains "a far better school system than I have seen in any comparable neighborhood." Stephen Phillips was the head of the largest district of small, self-governing schools of choice perhaps in the world— New York City's alternative high school division, home to dozens of innovative and acclaimed high schools—for over twenty years, serving many of the city's toughest students.

The experiences of these schools suggest that self-governance, choice, and smallness attract some extraordinarily good people and, what's more, enhance the work of otherwise quite ordinary people. The number of staff from East Harlem and from the alternative high school network that now play key leadership roles locally and nationally is extraordinary. Probably many either would still be classroom teachers or would have moved on to other careers had they not had the opportunity Alvarado and Phillips offered—to be in charge of shaping something truly interesting and different. Dozens of "ordinary" teachers rose to the challenge to design new schools. And many more probably would have, if the task had not required so much political perseverance and stamina in a bureaucratic climate that was still largely hostile to their missions. What made both the East Harlem and the New York alternative high school division's efforts blossom was the existence of support systems designed by Alvarado and Phillips that matched the task itself—flexible, responsive, always alert to ways to support the particular needs of each school. Just as a good classroom with high expectations transforms many ordinary kids, so too does a good school transform teachers and a good system transform its schools. The experience of these districts suggests that given the right context, the majority of ordinary teachers will bring new intellectual and moral energy to their schools. It's not just that "all children can learn"; almost all adults can too. And although there's no guarantee that all who can learn will do so, certain conditions increase the odds, and others decrease them.

Experiments in Scaling Up

The vision I've put forth here of trustworthy schools and school systems is, in other words, not all wishful thinking. I've been a participant in both of these "scaling up" efforts, starting with District 4 in the early seventies and the New York alternative high school division in the eighties. It was in the context of frustration over the absence of a citywide impact of our otherwise highly acclaimed high school work that six New York City alternative high school principals accepted the challenge: what would it take to make our work applicable to the city's larger reform agenda? The six schools, all affiliated with school reformer Ted Sizer's national Coalition of Essential Schools (CES), with support from several major foundations, designed a plan and made an offer.

The Coalition Campus School Project (CCSP), as the six CES schools called themselves, suggested that if the big impersonal failing high schools could be broken up into smaller schools, maybe they would work in a fashion similar to the existing small high schools. Given the immensity of the task of turning around schools with a long tradition of failure, why not give all schools a chance to start over—to redesign them from scratch? Maybe reinventing new schools within the physical plant of the old schools, with willing teachers and students who chose the place themselves, might undermine the habits of defeat and resistance that big failing schools had developed. And instead of requiring that they operate within the larger high school bureaucracy, provide a more intimate support structure. Maybe with the support of mentor schools that have gone through the same struggles they could avoid some of those schools' earlier mistakes.

We made the following proposal: Gradually close three big unquestionably failing high schools—one in each of the three most underperforming boroughs. Then gradually repopulate them as educational complexes housing five or six small CES-style schools for the same student population—schools modeled on the premises laid out in Ted Sizer's book *Horace's Compromise* and being practiced in the existing six successful CES schools. Establish formal mentoring ties between the new schools and the original six. Remodel some neighboring abandoned warehouses, factories, and office buildings so that sufficient additional space will exist for the growing student population, and so that the old buildings will be neither overcrowded nor exclusively havens for teenagers. The redesign of the old buildings would thus be able to serve a wider range of ages and services—high schools, middle schools, and schools for young children under one roof.

To our surprise, our proposal was accepted by the mayor, the state commissioner, the city chancellor, the school board, and the United Federation of Teachers in 1992. Selecting which schools to start with did not turn out to be the hard part, given the number of schools that met the criterion of eligibility: graduating less than a third of those who started out in ninth grade. While redesigning the old buildings, the project simultaneously needed to negotiate space and redesign nearby former office and warehouse spaces to hothouse the new small high schools, as the old high schools were phased out. We were not surprised that many colleagues in district and central offices were unsympathetic to the project or incompetent in working out all the exceptions required. That was expected. But even though we were often lacking diplomatic skills, once it was clear that the city's commitment was firm, we found that skeptical sympathizers emerged and converts appeared, if not in droves, in sufficient numbers to get the job done.

Within five years—from 1993 to 1998—the Manhattan site (the old Julia Richman High School) became a shining national example of the reuse of a large old-fashioned high school building to serve the same basic student population. The building now houses four independent high schools (including one exclusively for new immigrants), as well as an infant center, a kindergarten through eighth grade elementary and middle school, and a school for severely disabled youngsters. These schools coexist with three new small schools carved out of nearby downtown office buildings. Given the timing and the politics—both school and local—we were less successful in carrying out the second part of the project, the Bronx redesign of James Monroe High School, although the data are still comparatively promising. And we never made it to the third promised site in Brooklyn. Still, the very idea that people can take a large existing traditional high school and successfully refashion it into smaller schools serving the same original population has been validated.

Out of this work came some of the most detailed studies of school reform ever undertaken, conducted by Columbia University's National Center for Restructuring Education, Schools, and Teaching (NCREST), under Linda Darling-Hammond. The data proved that the project's goals were more than amply met—in terms of higher graduation rates, daily attendance, post–high school college attendance, and lower dropout rates. Data compiled in a court case against the state in defense of these schools noted that the New York high schools involved in the project "outpaced the citywide schools in the percentage of students going to four-year colleges and two-year colleges. Citywide, 62% of New York City high school students go on to college. Overall, 72% of the students in the small performance-based high school coalition that grew out of this work go on to college immediately upon graduation, and an additional 15–20% ultimately go on to college." This is especially impressive given that these schools' "overall dropout rate is half that of schools citywide." "At Urban Academy . . . at least 95% of every graduating class have been admitted to four year colleges. . . . Most Urban Academy students come from social and economic groups that have been historically underrepresented at American colleges. . . . On average, 40% are the first people in their families to attend college."

Above and beyond these statistics were the less obvious changes: greater parental participation (virtually all the parents in the new Bronx schools showed up for open house night), safety (Julia Richman High School soon got rid of its metal detectors). Per graduate, as a study by New York University proved, these small schools were less expensive to operate, although they cost slightly more per student.

In the second year of the CCSP project, in the fall of 1994, Walter

Annenberg approached Ted Sizer and the CES with an offer of up to
$50 million if we came up with a plan to make an impact on urban ed-
ucation. We were ready. We thought we knew how to invent good individual schools; we thought we knew how to turn around old failing
schools. But what would the system have to look like to make the continued existence of such schools, as well as their proliferation citywide,
easier and more long-lasting? Could the lessons of the alternative
superintendency and the CCSP become the city's modus operandi?
In short, what was needed to deal with the issue of public trust on a
large scale?

Reconceptualizing the Systemic: The Annenberg Project

Fueled by our past experience, the Coalition of Essential Schools,
plus three other experienced nonprofit school reform organizations,
joined forces to explore the idea. The four organizations differed on
many things—tactical, pedagogical, and ideological. But they agreed
on the three essentials: smallness, autonomy, and choice. The task
was to use our school-based experience to design a system compatible
with these essentials.

We consciously built in both new freedom and new methods of accountability. In return for more freedom over using their per capita
resources, hiring personnel, and organizing individual schools in their
particular ways, schools agreed to accept greater responsibility for
publicly demonstrating fiscal and educational accountability. We established a parallel experimental zone, with no particular geographic
boundaries, called a Learning Zone, to house our work. It would be
designed, at this stage, for no more than 5 percent of New York's
huge student population—over a hundred or so small schools citywide serving ultimately "only" fifty thousand students (out of 1.2 mil-
lion), subdivided into networks of four to seven schools and overseen
by a lean central office, ultimately accountable to the city's board of
education.

We weren't in this alone. The Annenberg Challenge gave a substantial boost to a wave of similar projects in cities across the country.

The work was fueled in part by the growing interest in vouchers and charters, but it was also driven by a commitment to public education and equity. By seeking a solution to the systemic through looking at the particular, different possibilities became thinkable—and heady. Maybe the best of the voucher idea could also be best for strengthening public education. We saw ourselves as collectively at the cutting edge. We were, to put it mildly, euphoric—if wary.

The Premises behind Another Way of Thinking

We knew that it was the particulars of each of our schools that lay at the heart of our surprising successes. It was their freedom of action that inspired the passions of those involved and drew upon the best in each of us. Rather than ignore such schools because their solutions lay in the particular talents and styles of utterly unreplicable individuals or circumstances, it's precisely such unreplicability that we knew needed to be celebrated and made systemic! What these special schools demonstrated to us is that every school must have the power and the responsibility to select and design its own particulars and thus surround all youngsters with powerful adults who are in a position to act on their behalf in open and publicly responsible ways. This was a way to better educate kids while simultaneously reeducating teachers. The key question for our systemic reform was how to support and hold accountable schools that were, on purpose, so very unalike? How to build a system compatible with good schooling rather than schools compatible with the existing system?

We began our work with five lessons.

1. Keep it simple. Our central office for the Learning Zone was tiny—we began with three people at maximum for the over fifty schools, maybe twenty-five thousand students, and twenty to twenty-five networks. We imposed very few reporting schemes. We used as our motto, with thanks to Satellite Academy principal Alan Dichter, "We're not going to tell you what to do, but it's not none of our business."

2. Be patient, and learn from experience. Add at most fifty new

schools over five years. (In a system with well over a thousand schools, it's easy to try to overreach.) We're aiming at a change that sticks, not another fad.

3. We're not ourselves always sure what and why certain practices work, so let's be sure to celebrate and honor variety within our midst, including interesting work outside our ranks, and be wary of talk about sacrificing some children's prospects in the present for the greater good of the many in the future. There are even some kids and families for whom particular big impersonal schools may be the most trustworthy.

4. Needed: a very lean master contract between the individual schools, the teachers' union, the city, and the state—covering the most basic obligations as well as those unwaivable local, state, and federal rules pertaining to health, safety, and equity.

5. We'll make mistakes. The price of mistakes is generally to add on a new rule, a new department, or a new monitoring device. Hold off! Watch and wait.

In exchange for such operational autonomy, we had to answer the legitimate demand to be accountable to the public. Did we know what we were doing, and did we have ways to prove our claims? In part the answer lay in the nature of the schools themselves. Smallness creates self-knowledge, self-governance allows for a range of voices now often missing, and choice permits disgruntled parents and teachers to vote with their feet. But while these three might undercut some of the pressure for more and more external and bureaucratic accountability, we knew it wouldn't be enough. Especially when we were working with families who had ample reason to distrust any school system. Without a powerful system of public accountability, well-intentioned individual schools can too easily become stuck in routines, parochial, smug, and secretive—even tyrannical, even racist. Dissidents, whether they come from the parent or teaching ranks, can become pariahs and eventually martyrs in the absence of a system of checks and balances, of places folks can go to complain or to check out their anecdotes against other forms of evidence. There were several different forms of public accountability that seemed to us not only compatible with but supportive of good school-based practice; so we wrote them into our plan for the Learning Zone.

Equity, student outcomes, and fiscal integrity were the bottom lines that we agreed to be held accountable for. Although we weren't required to prove we could manage any of these perfectly, we needed to produce evidence that we could manage them better than the existing alternate top-down schemes. We proposed four mechanisms of accountability:

1. *Judging student outcomes.* Aside from reporting on a lean list of standard common indicators, all our schools were committed to making their individual standards explicit, as well as the ways in which they measured student work toward meeting those standards. Four schools in our network—Central Park East Secondary School, Urban Academy, University Heights, and International High School—had pioneered distinct models that had already met with city and state approval as alternate approaches to meeting high school graduation standards. All four approaches enlisted college faculty members, parents, community members, and other high school teachers as part of an ongoing review of student work and faculty standards. Most of the new high schools adopted a variant of one of these four. A few stuck with more conventional accountability systems. Others began exploring some combination of traditional and nontraditional assessment systems.

2. *Mutual schoolwide oversight and assessment.* All our schools agreed to answer to one another for the quality of their work—to make themselves visible to their colleagues, to accept new forms of collegial oversight. Evidence from the experiences of private schools, other professions, and small businesses suggested that networks of like-minded enterprises might provide a vehicle for critical feedback. Organized properly, maybe schools could hold each other up to a mirror and ask, "Is this what you meant to be doing?" We proposed that all schools in the new Learning Zone be members of small learning networks of four to seven sister schools. Each network would organize a system of collective review of each other's work. No one best way was laid down; we figured this was an area where we'd do a lot of learning.

3. *Formal reviews.* We proposed formal review panels—public auditors—composed of both critical friends and more distanced and skeptical publics, to attest to the credibility of the networks, their mutual accountability systems, and the work of their schools—in terms of both quality and equity. It was such bodies that would demand convincing evidence that the network of schools under review was doing its job as promised, was acting responsibly. The findings of such review panels would be publicly available, and their recommendations ultimately the responsibility of the larger, democratically chosen public authorities—for example, the city's chancellor and central board.

4. *Collecting information and data.* Finally, everyone—teachers, parents, assessors, legislators, and the public at large—needed a shared body of credible and where possible longitudinal information (samples of actual student work and cohort studies, as well as statistical data) on which to build and test out their reflections and judgments about the work of the project. The funding for this must be a public responsibility. Without good data, we are all victims of public relations gurus and hype.

We had a vision, we had a rationale, and we had an accountability plan. Within a few months, the four educational reform organizations organized their schools into more than twenty self-chosen networks and began the work of the project, with plans for adding new schools each subsequent year.

Meanwhile that small lean central office, under the leadership of Douglas White—in collaboration with the New York University and NCREST (at Columbia's Teachers College) researchers—began to document the project's work. The researchers' task was to answer at least three questions: (1) Were kids, from all races and classes, doing well in such schools? (2) Did the project offer a promising direction for thinking about how small, self-governing schools of choice could be central to a system's reform strategy? (3) Could the project be sold to the larger public and policy-making communities? Although the proposed Learning Zone would encompass only about 5 percent of New York City's vast student population, it was right in the middle range of U.S. cities—about the size of Boston, Oakland, or

Washington, D.C. What was learned here might be easily translated elsewhere.

So, what went wrong?

The project floundered at this promising moment. The city's inability to keep the same chancellor for more than a few years, a change in state educational leadership after the election of a new governor, a shift in leadership on the local central school board, and a change in the local union's leadership all affected the continuity of an idea that was in itself not easy to grasp or summarize quickly—and was decidedly unusual. The four external supporting nonprofits also had their own differing agendas and their own turfs to protect in this time of shifting powers. To the new chancellor, most of the central office staff, as well as local district leaders faced with the reality of the redesign, the Learning Zone was threatening and risky. Only the union didn't blink. But fairly soon the Learning Zone was abandoned, and with it any officially sanctioned freedom in terms of rules and regulations as well as fiscal autonomy. This defeat led, in turn, to undermining the development of the accountability networks once the carrot of more freedom had been removed. What survived was a strengthened network of existing small schools. Not the dream, but a holding action.

These might have been temporary setbacks, part of any new bold venture. But something else was waiting in the wings—not just in New York but all across the nation—that would soon threaten the limited freedoms these schools had long enjoyed, not to mention the idea of expanding their reach. The advent of top-down standardization as the engine of reform was an idea diametrically opposite to the one animating the Annenberg proposal. The new reform wave suggested that what had been wrong was too loose a coupling of classrooms, schools, and central authorities, not one that was too tight. To reverse this problem, the new wave argued for centrally designed and measurable results with high-stakes penalties for failure to meet numeric testing goals—the granddaddy of all five-year plans.

Efforts at scaling up smallness would have to fall back on smaller-scale, less grandiose visions. Boston, for example, launched a similar approach in 1996 under the initiative of the local teachers' union—an intradistrict form of chartering. The Boston pilots, as they were called, of which Mission Hill was one, begun amid a flurry of excitement under one superintendent, were seen by the new superintendent as a sideline from which some good practices might be learned, but not systemic ones. Faced with new realities, the pilots soon became for the union a worry rather than an opportunity, as teachers in other schools were largely unexcited, if not threatened, by the pilots. In effect, the pilot proposal, with Annenberg support, met a fate similar to the one in New York City, except that the schools built in more freedom from the start and have not lost any since. Still, as in New York, the idea remains alive, and for example, in the winter of 2002 the faculty of one regular Boston high school—a first—voted overwhelmingly to go pilot. Thus the pilot schools continue to be a limited experiment in the idea that animated the New York City Annenberg project.

Throughout the country, at other Annenberg sites, comparable efforts were begun with comparable promising but limited results. Chicago had a major small schools network as part of its Annenberg grant and launched several dozen promising new schools at the same moment that Chicago turned 180 degrees, from being the pioneer of school-based decision making to a model of centralized power. Not surprisingly, all the existing Annenberg sites were also tempted by apparently easier solutions that did not threaten to change the locus of power, or that placed power in politically more powerful locations— mayors, governors, or civic elites. The trend was to solve the accountability issue by building systems that placed power further and further from the action, not closer—largely through the adoption of one or another high-stakes standardized test to replace local or professional judgments. The rationale was often not educational but frankly political—as the only way to get strong business support behind reform— and thus behind needed funds. But in city after city, support for small schools with greater autonomy also has proved irresistible. Oakland is the latest to redesign its system to accommodate smallness on a large scale. The Annenberg work, like the current new infusion of funds for small schools from the Gates Foundation in a number of major urban areas (including Massachusetts, Seattle, the Bay Area, and New York), helps keep the small schools momentum from disappearing, although it's a constant battle to survive until the wheel once again returns to a greater interest in site-based empowerment.

The new consensus, that the change agents must come from outside, uninfected by intimate knowledge of schools, kids, or families—and with enough clout to overcome local resistance—made holding on, not scaling up, the order of the day for small schools. Ironically, ten years after the first efforts by the CCSP to dismantle the old high schools, New York City offered to give failing big schools away to private bidders. They even offered to give the privateers more public money than we raised from private funders to remodel Julia Richman or James Monroe rather than follow the CCSP or Annenberg model. (At the moment, the giveaway has fortunately been stalled owing to parental opposition.) The lack of follow-through on the CCSP work was not because it was demonstrated that the program couldn't work, but because it required a fundamental shift in the way we do business that the school systems and their powerful allies within the business and political world weren't ready to embark on. (Although on a far smaller scale, the Learning Zone idea we proposed was in fact instituted six years later to enable several charter schools that had been part of the original small schools movement to return to the city system and retain their autonomy. Eric Nadelstern, the director of one of them, has been asked to transform all the Bronx high schools into small schools, without extra resources or clout, but it's hard to not try—again and again.)

There's no way to guarantee that any particular system will work, or will work forever, or will not need endless revising. But until we get over the idea that there is a one-size-fits-all solution to schools, above all for schools that are trustworthy enough to do the job well, we won't allow ourselves to do the difficult long-term work of redesigning the system, not just the schools. What we need is a new kind of system whose central task is to protect the public space needed for innovation. We need a lean, mean system, with a limited but critical accountability function, to be the guardian of our common public interest, but one that respects the fact that schools must be first and foremost responsive to their own constituents—the members of their community—not to the system. That's the rub.

At times this idea seems utopian even to me. Do we imagine that all our fellow human beings are wise, good, and competent? Can we trust them? Our immediate instinct is to write pages of "what ifs" and "supposing thats" to protect ourselves from the abuses that are bound to arise as ordinary people struggle to make their ideas work in ordinary contexts. But the alternatives, one or another version of what we all know too well or the elimination of public education itself—proposed by some who believe only the unfettered marketplace can do the job—are even more utopian. On the hopeful side, it's well to remind ourselves that the majority of the public is, actually, surprisingly trustful of the public schools they know best—their own children's schools or those in their own community. According to a recent *Education Week*/PEN poll, 70 percent of those with kids in schools give the school their eldest child attends an A or a B. And 56 percent—parents and nonparents—give such a grade to all the schools in their community.

In short, Americans are more, not less, positive about the schools we actually have than I am! In some ways, that's why so many of my friends supported the impulse behind the crisis charges against public education throughout the eighties and nineties—they hoped that a too trustful public would wake up to what schools could be, rather than settling for what they actually were. Distrust didn't just happen.

But this language of crisis has backfired, leaving the majority of the public open to the belief that—at least with respect to those schools far removed from their own community—there "ought to be a law," some systemic, single powerful lever that will get everyone working up to snuff without spending a lot more on doing anything substantially different. I am suggesting, instead, that we need to bite the bullet and accept that there is neither a perfect answer nor any way we can legislate it into being. And the answers aren't cheap.

Trust has its drawbacks and won't always be warranted, but properly skeptical distrust should lead us to closer ties between the community and the school, not looser ones, facing the root of the distrust, not running for the protection of far-removed authorities and experts. Trying to create the kind of trustworthy schools I propose will have its troubles, but it will also have a chance to stack the deck in favor of learning for all the nation's children.

CHAPTER TEN

Democracy and
Public Education

As I drive about the neighborhood looking for ideas for my summer garden in upstate New York, I'm struck by the meticulously cared for and obviously beloved gardens that don't appeal to me, some that are attractive but not me, not to mention some that seem ugly and tasteless. The teacherly instinct is also at times the dictator's instinct—to make everyone be like me. I want to rearrange their gardens. To pass a law. But, then, part of the pleasure I take in my own garden is its uniqueness. First of all, my garden fits my terrain, with its constraints, both good and bad—the rocky hillside, the pond beyond the fir trees, the huge maples hovering overhead, the barn off in the distance, with the fields and rolling hills spreading out beyond it. I need a garden suited to this setting. But also the garden suits my desire for a particular kind of effect; I want it to look almost as though no one had planned it. I want it to seem somewhat wild and untamed, with an occasional oasis that was clearly planned to the last detail, just to show that I could do it if I wanted to. And just as I flinch at what someone else thought of as beautiful, I can imagine some are probably offended by my taste or, more likely, just assume I didn't have the time or energy to clean it all up and make it look like a real garden.

I watch visitors to our school, and I detect some too polite to say aloud what they are privately wondering: "What's going on here? This isn't a 'real' school." They too must imagine how nice it would be to clean it all up and make it look like it should.

So while I know that what we need in a democratic society are schools that vary, that suit our tastes—more or less—I also know how hard it is to keep our hands off each other's schools. And unlike gardens, schooling is not something one can take or leave. In the modern world it occupies too central a place in the raising of our children and our fellow citizens to assume we can either let others decide what it will be like or accept one central authority's taste for what the one best model ought to be. The temptation to pass a law is far greater, and far more understandable.

We need to accept the public responsibility of seeing all our children as our common responsibility, while at the same time avoiding the arrogance of thinking there is therefore only one right way. It's not a question of asking schools to eschew values or renounce the vigorous defense of particular points of view. On the contrary. I believe we need to keep the door open to the varied ways such values can be expressed in a democratic society. Ideally most of these differences can take place simultaneously within a network of neighborhood-controlled public schools.

But variety needs to be balanced by the acknowledgment that there exists a larger community—one we all have a stake in—a shared public. The balkanization of our civic life is not an unreal fear or without danger. If variety, after all, were the only goal, why keep schools public? Why not let the market do the job of guaranteeing diversity? (In fact, our experience with marketplace competition suggests that it too prefers standardized solutions and offers diversity only when there's a small niche market that offers a sufficiently greater profit.)

For me the most important answer to the question "Why save public education?" is this: It is in schools that we learn the art of living together as citizens, and it is in public schools that we are obliged to defend the idea of a public, not only a private, interest.

Debates, for instance, over what constitutes appropriate or inappropriate play yard behavior and how best to punish wrongdoers are mirrors of our larger social struggles over what being a good citizen is and over what justice should look like. Schools are where we learn about the possible meanings of patriotism—what it means to own one's community and have a stake in its reputation. How much more tenuous such relationships are when schools become huge, their decision-making apparatus invisible or far distant, and when citizens no longer feel connected to their children's schools. In only slightly over half a century we've gone from having two hundred thousand school boards to fewer than twenty thousand—serving at least twice as many youngsters.

It is within schools that we can learn how to live with such uneasy balances, even cherish them—even as we naturally are often averse to doing so! The odds must be stacked against any too easy escape from the annoyances of our fellow citizens. It's within our schools, and in the governance of them, that we need to learn how to resist institutional and peer pressures, as well as respect the institutions we live with and the peers who are our fellow citizens. It's in such institutions that we need to learn to handle authority in all its many forms—both legitimate and illegitimate—and how to take authority on—effectively. It's within such schools that we need to learn to resist what we see as improper encroachments on our rights, and to organize and expand what we believe to be our entitlements. All the habits of mind and work that go into democratic institutional life must be practiced in our schools until they truly become habits—so deeply a part of us that in times of stress we fall back on them rather than abandon them in search of a great leader or father figure, or retreat into the private isolation of our private interests, the unfettered marketplace where one need not worry about the repercussions of one's individual decisions.

Like the learning of all important things, the learning of these democratic habits of mind happens only when children are in the real company of adults they trust and when adults have sufficient powers—and the leisure—to be good company. On the largest political scale, this is why I worry so much about—and work so hard to change—the way children are growing up without adult company, a

community of elders. In some ways we accept our children's adulthood long before we once did, and in other ways we continue to treat
them as children for far longer. We fear for them as we never did before, thus protecting them from independent play before and after
school, and restricting even the kind of play they once engaged in at
lunch and recess. Thus, while school occupies only a fifth of kids' waking hours, the institutions we've invented for the rest of the day are
remarkably similar—only for many kids far shabbier and less well
funded. And in the time left over, the mass media provide a highly
compelling world for the young, who spend considerably more time
watching the screen than talking to any adults. And, of course, they
sneak off together in packs to browse around their favorite meeting
places, shopping malls, where they are, once again, consumers amid
strangers whom surely they would be wise not to trust.

The consequences of our interpersonal estrangement are not obvious, even as there is a growing literature on the topic, and I quite
frankly am only beginning my exploration. I don't know what all this
means in terms of personality development, neurosis, stress, illness,
intimacy, and long-term relationship building. There may even be
some positives that we will learn to celebrate and nourish. But I do
think I begin to see dangerous signs of what such estrangement does
to the creation of potentially viable democratic communities.

Democracy assumes the prior existence of communities of people with shared loyalties, confidences, and understandings. It doesn't
create them—they are far older and more persistent than modern (or
even ancient) democracies. We have always taken such communities
for granted. They were an inevitable byproduct of being human beings. What got me nervous was the erosion of such naturally forming
communities—or at least their formation in ways quite different than
we as humans have ever known before. It's not always easy to know
when something new is merely a new wrinkle or a dangerous break-
down of civilization. Crisis talk always worries me, so I say this with
trepidation.

It was in becoming a high school principal that I first noticed what
was unusual: the absence of interest on the part of so many adoles-

cents in the world of adults; the isolation of adolescents from relationships with anyone much different—above all in age and experience —from themselves; the lack of a sense of membership in any larger society that could be appealed to. At first I just thought of this phenomenon as it related to my unusual attachment for the adult world as a youngster—my hurry to grow up and join the big world. I also knew that grown-ups have a habit of seeing each generation through jaundiced eyes, and I hardly wanted to sign on to that sorry habit. I tended, in fact, to pooh-pooh claims about this generation being different from. . . . But it struck me—in a way, very suddenly—that there was something new abroad. The vast majority of kids were spending an incredibly critical period of their lives, forming their relationship with the world, in the most bizarre way; never in the history of the species did one think of raising the young to become adults in the absence of the company of adults. And, above all, in the absence of adults whom children imagined becoming, or—and here was the key—whom children even knew well enough to imagine trusting. I also noticed that this isolation was happening at an earlier and earlier age. But the closer kids came to being adults, the fewer adults they encountered.

And never has it been more important that we learn how to relate to people we don't automatically trust, who aren't kin or otherwise obvious allies, but strangers we must deal with "as if" we trusted each other, as if being human itself was ground for respect. Because while probably all human civilizations require some such mutuality, democracy lives off of that "as if"—the quality of trust is central to democracy. This is also why, until very modern times, few societies opted for democracy without first enormously limiting who was included— people "like us." A democratic society's need for both skepticism regarding others and empathy for them is surely easier to meet when one's fellow citizens are not too different from oneself.

But modern democratic and pluralistic societies require trust even when their members are, in fact, very different from each other. We need to be able to count on each other most of the time to act "as if" we were trustworthy, even as we also know that we will often enough have our trust betrayed. We are shocked (naively?) by politicians' machinations to undermine the democratic process. But much as we must learn from such betrayals, we need to learn to cope with them in ways that neither abandon the idea of democracy nor undermine our sense of community. We still need to assume that it is not beyond reason to view the world as more or less trustworthy—that things can make some sense, including both those natural phenomena that so often seem puzzling and the many equally perplexing human relationships. I fall back on Winston Churchill's pithy reminder that democracy may well be "the worst form of government except for all the other forms which have been tried from time to time."

We need to know the nature of the connections between ourselves and the planet, to test out our powers over the material world, to recognize our limitations; we need to know when to sit back and get pleasure from the world we didn't make—as we gradually understand better and acknowledge its ultimate unknowability. So too with our connections to our fellow beings, who are equally unknowable in any ultimate sense. We cannot actually "be" others; we can only stretch our well-informed imaginations. This is what many scientists remind me is at the heart of a good science education: allowing kids time to play with the world, lie back in awe to take in the sky, dig holes to China, watch the dominoes topple over and over and over again.

Modern life requires an appreciation for the complexity and interconnectedness of people and other living things, if we have any hope of maintaining both the planet and our democratic institutions. And since those are my hopes, I'm counting a lot on our ability to build a system of schooling that helps reforge such connections.

Many of the stories in this book can, from this perspective, be seen as stories about schools as crucibles of democratic life. Akwasi's public and civil argument with me—the principal—over the graphing requirements of his mathematics portfolio is a lesson in democracy. The dissatisfied parents whom I'm obliged to confront in our communal office at times not always convenient to me, the parents and students who use the photocopier without asking, the students who expect that the government of the school should be visible to them, the students who put notes in my mailbox about issues they want to be addressed at our next staff meeting are all examples of people, in real institutions, sending messages about what one has a right to expect from society and what one is responsible to give back to it as well. In far too many schools, neither parents nor students seem to know who makes decisions or how they are made. Of course, increasingly, no one in the school is deciding anything of importance. The important decisions are being made in places far removed—in state boards and central offices—with good citizenship defined only as the task of implementing and complying.

It's just a plain ornery fact (whether we like it or not) that no two living things are exactly alike. By creating a way of thinking about schooling that allows for, even enjoys and relishes, some of the most fantastic of differences, we might encourage the same for society writ large. Schooling can help us build strong images of the kinds of habits needed to keep pluralistic aspirations alive, for my grandchildren's grandchildren's grandchildren. If democratic habits can't flourish in school, if they are viewed as utopian in the place we should have the most reasons for trusting each other, how much harder to believe in their possibility in society at large? Continuity, predictability, and the mundane needs of today go hand in hand with big dreams—but only if we are heedful of the tensions that arise between our dreams and daily realities. This is what human-scaled schools are best able to do.

Of course, when all is said and done, I suspect I'm hanging on to this viewpoint because I like the fact that we are by nature unique, unpredictable, complex, never fully knowable, and endlessly varied. I'm glad that the real world doesn't come with built-in multiple-choice boxes, precoded and ready to score. I'm delighted when the storm clouds gather overhead, just when I thought the endless blueness was there for keeps. They are a reminder of the possibility that nature—including human nature—has something surprising in store for me. The thing that keeps me going, on even the gloomiest of days, is that element of potential surprise. Who knows what's around the corner? I recognize that my response to the unpredictable might be the byproduct of having been raised in a safe and secure environment where surprises were more likely to be good than bad. Perhaps. But that's what I want for all kids. An openness to surprise is perhaps part of that magical resiliency that researchers are always looking for to explain how some are better or worse at coping with adversity. Here is one contribution to the future that good schools can offer. Schools can be places where we learn what it might be like if life were seen as almost always at least interesting, where the surprises facing us—adults and kids—are likely to be good ones, and where the occasional bad surprise can often be reframed, reorganized to make it easier to handle. And even when the unexpected is truly and inescapably hurtful, schools can be places for healing—if we are surrounded by people we have reason, however cautiously, to trust. Such schools could be the kind of community that the boys described in chapter 1 were seeking, a place where they could invent their own lives, but also a place deeply connected to the lives of trusted adults.

SUGGESTED READINGS

The following are some of the sources I examined as I thought about this book. I began by hoping to note just a few in each category, but I kept adding "just one more." This is a way to share with readers where my ideas come from and what I think is out there that supports, deepens, or even raises troubling questions about the ideas and proposals put forth in this book—but it's only a rough sample and includes, for example, no Dewey or Piaget.

I. Small Schools: Stories about Creating Small Learning Communities

William Ayers, Michel Klonsky, and Gabrielle Lyons, eds. *A Simple Justice: The Challenge of Small Schools.* Teachers College Press, 2000. Includes essay on race and class by Pedro Noguerra, on small schools efforts of the past, including Mississippi's freedom schools, and some important new small schools (including an essay by me).

Evans Clinchy, ed. *Transforming Public Education* (1997), *Reforming American Education from the Bottom to the Top* (1999), *Creating New Schools: How Small Schools Are Changing American Education.* Heinemann, 2000. Collected essays by leading practitioners on efforts to build small trustworthy communities.

David Bensman. *Central Park East and Its Graduates.* Teachers College Press, 2000. A revised and updated account, including stories and interviews—plus statistics—on what happened to the first few graduating classes at CPE.

Linda Darling-Hammond, Jacqueline Ancess, and Susanna Wichterle Ort. "An Account of the Coalition Campus Schools Project." *Reinventing High School,* Winter 2002. An independent documentation of the first three years of the work to reinvent Julia Richman High School in New York City, with lots of data. It's a good look at the insides of reform efforts.

Carl Glickman. *Democracy in Education.* Jossey-Bass, 1998. Analytic and descriptive story of important work going on to build the same kind of communities this book describes; set largely in rural Georgia.

Laraine K. Hong. *Surviving School Reform: A Year in the Life of One School.* Teachers College Press, 1996. A brutally revealing personal account of the cost often paid by those in the field for taking each new school reform swing seriously—time after time.

Jane Kern. *Inventing a School.* Sentry Press, 1999. A small Florida community, but lots of the details are reminiscent of our struggles in a big city! One of many such accounts—these ventures are not so rare after all.

Elliot Levine. *One Kid at a Time: Big Lessons from a Small School.* Teachers College Press, 2001. An account of the work of a network of high schools led by Dennis Littky that has broken new ground when it comes to rethinking schools that make a difference.

Dorothy Peters. *Taking Cues from Kids.* Heinemann, 2000. A lively exchange of letters with student teachers Peters supervised at Central Park East as they sought to make sense of the new and different; a look at the details of what surprised them.

Susan Semel and Alan Sadovnik, eds. *"Schools of Tomorrow," Schools of Today.* Peter Lang, 1999. Chapters on eleven public and private schools of yesterday and today that are examples of "progressive" education—including a chapter on several New York City schools that I know well.

Gregory Smith, ed. *Public Schools That Work: Creating Community.* Routledge, 1993. An account of a half dozen schools that sought to break the mold and the implications of their work. Chapters are largely by practitioners.

Tony Wagner. *Making the Grade: Reinventing America's Schools.* Routledge-Falmer, 2001. Tony has been looking closely at reform for the past twenty years; this one and *How Schools Change* (Beacon) describe his take on key issues facing reform.

Pat Wasley and others. *Small Schools, Great Strides.* Bank Street College of Education, 2000. Focuses on work in Chicago, looks at a wide range of data to make sense of the success of Chicago's small schools work over the past decade.

Pat Wasley, Robert Hampel, and Richard Clark. *Kids and School Reform.* Jossey-Bass, 1997. Firsthand material on how kids respond to changing the norms of schooling as we usually know them, and what the authors have found are the essentials that make a difference.

Joel Westheimer. *Among School Teachers: Community, Autonomy, and Ideology in Teachers' Work.* Teachers College Press, 1998. Westheimer meticulously describes two schools seeking to be communities and the differences and difficulties involved.

George H. Wood. *A Time to Learn: The Story of One High School's Transformation.* Dutton, 1998. A colleague whose work I've always admired tells the story of making dramatic changes in a one-school town in Ohio. Also see *Schools That Work* (Penguin, 1992), which includes a chapter on Central Park East Secondary School.

Fred Wiseman, *High School II.* Zipporah Films, Cambridge, Mass. A 3 1/2-hour documentary film about Central Park East Secondary School. Full of wonderful scenes that capture how people relate to each other—parents, teachers, kids.

II. Accounts of Urban Schooling and School Reform

Roland S. Barth. *Learning by Heart.* Jossey-Bass, 2001. A wise account and a how-to on the dilemmas facing school reformers at the turn of this century, by one who has watched a lot of reformers get stuck along the way. See also *Improving Schools from Within* (Jossey-Bass, 1990), a more optimistic account written before "standards."

Gerald Bracey writes regular columns for the *Phi Delta Kappan* and does an annual survey of education for a relentless reminder of the real data. He's funny and biting.

John Chubb and Terry Moe. *Politics, Markets, and American Schools.* Brookings Institution, 1990. A good description of what's wrong with public systems, even if I don't agree with their solution—privatization and vouchers.

James Comer. *School Power.* Free Press, 1980; revised edition, 1995. Focused on reform through community and parental involvement, Comer addresses issues of power within schools and the impact on student achievement. Based on hands-on work in schools.

Raymond Damonico. *Appraising Walter Annenberg's Gift to Public Education: Case Study of New York City.* The Thomas R. Fordham Foundation, 2000. Two revealing and quite accurate chapters describe the ambitious NYC effort at systemic small schools reform. An important piece of history told vividly and well.

Collin Greer. *The Great School Legend.* Basic Books, 1972. A good place to start when one gets discouraged. A classic reminder of whom American public schools never educated well.

David Kirp. *Almost Home.* Princeton University Press, 1995. Explores our mixed messages about community, with an account of how schools work for and against such aspirations. There's a great chapter on District 4 in East Harlem that manages to be usefully critical, in the best sense.

Jonathon Kozol. *Savage Inequalities.* HarperCollins, 1991. In the past ten years these inequalities have only gotten worse, but we seem less, not more, indignant. On a more optimistic note, reread Kozol's *Death at an Early Age* (Houghton Mifflin, 1967) about Boston forty years ago—some things have changed for the better.

Ann Lieberman, ed. *Building a Professional Culture in Schools.* Teachers College Press, 1988. A longtime student of teacher culture puts together some of the more important essays in the field of professional development and teacher education.

Donna Muncey and Patrick McQuillan. *Reform and Resistance in Schools and Classrooms.* Yale University Press, 1998. A study of the Coalition of Essential Schools efforts—school-by-school ethnographic case studies of successes and failures.

Neil Postman. *The End of Education.* Knopf, 1995. Asks the big question: why? His elegantly posited answers could help initiate a needed argument.

Art Powell, David Cohen, and Eleanor Farrar. *The Shopping Mall High School.* Houghton Mifflin, 1985. Well-written essays that explain how we got to the big impersonal high school and what it does to kids and their learning. A classic.

Richard Rothstein. *The Way We Were? The Myths and Realities of American Student Achievement.* Century Foundation Report, 1998. Rothstein's classic needs to be read and reread frequently—maybe nightly, for humor and perspective.

Seymour Sarason. *The Predictable Failure of School Reform.* Jossey-Bass, 1990. One of Sarason's many books, all of them musts. I spent a summer reading and rereading this one, determined to prove him wrong. Not yet.

Theodore Sizer. *Horace's Hope.* Houghton Mifflin, 1996. I recommend this one in particular for the chapter on scaling up, especially in connection with my own on that topic. It's a great summary of a complex topic.

David Tyack. *The One Best System.* Harvard University Press, 1974. An important overview of what's been happening in America's schools for the past century.

David Tyack and Larry Cuban. *Tinkering toward Utopia: A Century of Public School Reform.* Harvard University Press, 1995. Both authors have done important work putting current efforts in perspective. The best big, long-range history I know of.

Cornel West. Videotape of speech on education, plus written copy. The national office of Coalition of Essential Schools has the videotape and printed copy of a speech West made in the fall of 2000 that both inspires and unsettles me. (Look at other titles by West for useful and relevant material on schooling and race.)

Arthur E. Wise. *Legislated Learning: The Bureaucratization of the American Classroom*. University of California Press, 1979. Nothing new under the sun—we've been at this love affair with centralized planning for a long time.

III. On Testing, Standards, and Ways to Think about Assessment

Ron Berger. *The Culture of Standards*. Providence, R. I.: Annenberg Institute, 1996. The best brief for a different view of standards, by an extraordinary classroom teacher and colleague; should be put into every school board member's hands when anyone says "standards."

Gerald W. Bracey. *Bail Me Out!* Corwin Press, 2000. Great for getting behind those statistics, including test score data. A must source book.

Linda Darling-Hammond, Jacqueline Ancess, and Beverly Falk. *Authentic Assessment in Action*. Teachers College Press, 1995. Documented assessment practices in successful urban schools. Most were also published separately by Columbia's NCREST, a center led by Darling-Hammond. For example, *Graduation by Portfolio at Central Park East Secondary School*. New York: NCREST, 1994.

Fairtest. *Standardized Tests and Our Children* (30 pages) and *Implementing Performance Assessment* (60 pages). Two of many published by the only organization in the United states, and maybe the world, devoted to keeping the testing industry honest. Also see http:/www.fairtest.org for conversations among critics of testing, their newsletter, and information about Fairtest's work.

Stephen Jay Gould. *The Mismeasure of Man*. Norton, 1981. A best current history and explanation of why efforts to scientifically rank humans by intelligence don't work.

Lani Guinier and Susan Sturm. *Who's Qualified?* Beacon Press, 2001. The authors examine the evidence and conclude that test scores do not predict what they claim to. A provocative analysis of how else we might measure "merit."

Walter Haney. *The Myth of the Texas Miracle in Education*. Education Policy Analysis Archives, vol. 8, no. 41, August 19, 2000. http://epaa.asu.edu/epaa/vn41/ Access by date. Detailed statistical analysis of what really happened in Texas. Also, *Lakewoebeguaranteed; Misuse of Test Scores in Massachusetts*. Education Policy Analysis Archives (http://epaa.asu.edu/epaa/), 2002. A brilliant analysis of how MCAS is designed and scored, which I didn't read until after this book was finished or I'd have had even more ammunition.

Richard J. Herrnstein and Charles Murray. *The Bell Curve: Intelligence and Class Structure in American Life.* Free Press, 1994. Good to reread occasionally, when one thinks that racism went out of fashion long ago. This book became a center of serious debate—and serious praise—a mere seven years ago—and not just among right-wing racist kooks.

Banesh Hoffmann. *The Tyranny of Testing.* Collier Press, 1964. An oldie. It's still a great read and, as noted in chapter 6, it was Hoffman who got me going on my crusade against testing!

Harold Howe II. *Thinking about Our Kids.* Free Press, 1992. One of the most eminent of scholar/activists (former commissioner of education), with a great short chapter on measurement.

Thomas Johnson. *Profit beyond Measure.* Free Press, 2000. A noted accounting theorist examines, based on the successful experience of Toyota, the advantages of business practices that focus on decentralized data under the control of those who know what it represents firsthand.

Alfie Kohn. *The Case against Standardized Testing: Raising the Scores, Ruining the Schools.* Heinemann, 2000. An impassioned, funny, clear, and well-reasoned critique of the current madness.

Linda McNeil. *Contradictions of School Reform: Educational Costs of Standardized Testing.* Routledge, 2000. A good account of the realities of testing reform in Texas; to be supplemented by reading Walter Haney on the same topic.

Deborah Meier et al. *Will Standards Save Public Education?* Beacon Press, 2000. My response to the very idea of a single "approved" set of standards about what it means to be well educated. With responses from friends and foes: Bill Ayers, Abigail Thernstrom, Linda Nathan, Bob Chase, Ted Sizer, Gary Nash, and Richard Murname, plus a foreword by Jonathon Kozol.

L. Scott Miller. *An American Imperative: Accelerating Minority Educational Achievement.* Yale University Press, 1991. Miller's relentless questions helped me think about race, class, and testing in the early years of Central Park East Secondary School, when Miller was working for the Exxon Educational Fund.

Susan Ohanian. *One Size Fits Few.* Heinemann, 1999. A pleasurable read (anything by Ohanian is worth it) that takes standardized testing over the coals—with lots of down-to-earth examples and a strong sense of humor.

Vito Perrone. An unpublished manuscript on standardized testing, written in 1999, is one of the best treatments I've ever read on the subject. I hope it will soon be available more widely.

W. James Popham. *The Truth about Testing.* Association of Supervision Curriculum Development (ASCD), 2001. One of the leading testing experts takes a look at what it's all about—and comes to some startling conclusions—it's not about school achievement.

Diane Ravitch. *National Standards in American Education: A Citizen's Guide.* Brooking Institute, 1995. Ravitch shares my preference for small schools freed from bureaucracy—but she's also for top-down standards and national testing.

Peter Sacks. *Standardized Minds.* Perseus Books, 1999. A sound and thorough look at the impact of testing from a critic who comes out pretty much where I do on these issues.

Theodore Sizer. *Horace's Compromise, Horace's Hope, Horace's School.* Houghton Mifflin, 1985. Classics on standards versus standardization. Readable, down-to-earth, close to the life of the classroom—and profound. Sizer changed the conversation about schooling.

Claude Steele. "Thin Ice: A Three-Part Series." *Atlantic Monthly,* August 1999. Helps shed light on the "achievement gap" in test scores, with thoughts about what might be done to undercut the impact of stereotype threats on test results.

Marc S. Stucker and Judith B. Codding. *Standards for Our Schools: How to Set Them, Measure Them, and Reach Them.* Jossey-Bass, 1998. A detailed defense of the idea of national standards and ways in which they can and are being carried out in many schools and school districts in America by two of the most sensible proponents (meaning closest to me on other criteria) of standardized and measurable standards. This still seems to me the best defense of what I disagree with.

Thomas Wilson. *Reaching for a Better Standard: How English Inspection Provokes the Way Americans Know and Judge Schools.* Teachers College Press, 1996. A detailed account of a promising approach to public review of school achievement, not uncommon among private schools and increasingly being favored for public education.

Videos: *Graduation by Portfolio,* produced by Judith Gold; *Urban Academy's Graduation Process,* videotaped by Ann Cook; *The Mission Hill Graduation Process,* by Heidi Lyne. Just three of many video accounts of alternative approaches to maintaining public standards. For more information on their availability contact the Coalition of Essential Schools in Oakland or the author.

IV. On Teaching, Learning, and Growing Up

Ann Berlak and Sekani Moyenda. *Taking It Personally: Racism in the Classroom.* Temple University Press, 2001. An important account from two close observers, white and black, of some of the ways race plays itself out in schools and why it hurts.

Patricia Carini. *Starting Strong.* Teachers College Press, 2001. Carini's work and the work of the Prospect Center have been an important and critical outpost for keeping our focus on children and the meaning of their work. An earlier work, *The School Lives of Seven Children: A Five-Year Study*, published by University of North Dakota in Grand Forks in 1982 is a must-read also.

Edward Chittenden and Terry Salinger, with Ann Bussis. *Inquiry Into Meaning.* Teachers College Press, 2001. This revised classic, is one of the few books on reading that starts with the learner and tries to do for reading research what linguists finally did to understand the learning of oral language, by going to the child in the act of learning.

Gerald Coles. *Misreading Reading: The Bad Science That Hurts Children.* Heinemann, 2000. A good, well-documented reminder about how the current fad to substitute bad "science" for serious, thoughtful understanding can hurt our kids. Read it alongside the Chittenden book noted above.

James Comer. *Maggie's American Dream.* New American Library, 1988. An important historical reminder of the background of today's struggles, from a personal perspective.

Linda Darling-Hammond. *The Right to Learn.* Jossey-Bass, 1997. You might as well start here with Linda Darling-Hammond if you haven't already been following her ideas and projects. This book outlines the critical "inputs"—what it requires—to take seriously all the talk about closing gaps and educating children "as children."

Lisa Delpit. *Other People's Children.* New Press, 1996. Still a classic on what it means to be a teacher or learner of "other people's" children; provocative, good reading, and appropriately disturbing. Look for essays by Delpit on related topics in a variety of publications.

Eleanor Duckworth. *The Having of Wonderful Ideas.* Teachers College Press, 1996. There is no other to match it, so I recommend it whenever I can. It's my "bible"—a reminder of what learning means.

David Elkind. *The Hurried Child.* Addison-Wesley, 1981. This classic sums up a lot of the issues of child-rearing that closely relate and tie together with issues facing us in school.

Eric Erickson. *Childhood and Society.* Norton, 1963. Erikson's seminal work on the stages of childhood beginning with the role of trust in childhood remained in my mind throughout the writing of this book.

Robert Fried. *The Passionate Teacher* and *The Passionate Learner.* Beacon, 1996 and 2001, respectively. How-to guide books for teachers and parents, provocative essays on why this kind of teaching and learning matters, and just inspirational.

Samuel G. Freedman. *Small Victories.* HarperCollins, 1990. Freedman manages to do what the subtitle suggests, make real "the world of a teacher, her students, and their high school." He helps us see why Jessica Siegel loved her work, why it worked.

Howard Gardner. *The Unschooled Mind: How Children Think and How Schools Should Teach.* Basic Books, 1991. An older classic, to read alongside his newest and latest; reminders of how far we've slipped from remembering what the purpose of schooling is.

Paul Goodman. *Compulsory Miseducation.* Random House, 1964. To be reread every ten years, forever. Strong, thoughtful, controversial, and provocative essay by one of our great iconoclastic thinkers on the state of youth in America. Still rings true nearly forty years later.

Maxine Greene. *The Dialectic of Freedom.* TC Press, 1988. Try chapter 2, "Freedom, Education, and Public Spaces." But, of course, try anything by and about this philosopher, who has kept her eyes on our schools and classrooms and the values they do and don't teach.

James Herndon. *The Way It Spozed to Be.* Bantam, 1969. Aside from being a classic about teaching told from inside the classroom, it's a great story about the difficulties of reform. All his books—written more than thirty years ago—should be reread with both themes in mind.

Thomas Hine. *The Rise and Fall of the American Teenager.* Avon, 2000. A useful history that helped me ground my own thoughts—what was nostalgia versus reality?

John Holt. *How Children Fail.* Dell, 1968. An old classic that changed my life.

Alfie Kohn. *The Schools We Deserve* (Mariner, 2000) and *Punishment by Reward* (Houghton Mifflin, 1993). Our most eminent gadfly, activist, and indefatigable investigator of what matters in the raising of good and thoughtful children. Pick anything he has written.

Robert Moses. *Radical Equations: Civil Rights from Mississippi to the Algebra Project.* Beacon Press, 2001. A reminder of how education can be "civil rights" work of the highest order. Moses also gets down to the practical details of how to translate this into mathematical literacy.

Jennifer Obidah and Karen Markheim Teel. *Because of the Kids: Facing Racial and Cultural Differences in School.* TC Press, 2001. A white teacher and an African American colleague tackle the particulars of schoolhouse racism. Their courage and tenacity to tackle the daily life of Karen's classroom was at times painful to read.

Clara Claiborne Park. *Exiting Nirvana: A Daughter's Life with Autism.* Little, Brown, 2001. In this particular and beautifully recounted story, one relearns a lot about the role of human relationships—and the critical importance for both social and intellectual life—that the capacity for empathy plays in human development.

David Perkins. *Smart Schools: Better Thinking and Learning for Every Child.* Free Press, 1992. One of our most distinguished educational and learning theoristscovers "the waterfront" about the relationship between schooling and learning.

Vito Perrone. *A Letter to Teachers*. Jossey-Bass, 1991. He has not written many
books but influences mostly by his presence, his advice, his active engagement with the world of schooling. If you don't know him that way, this
book will give you a sense why he has been so important to so many teachers.

Mike Rose. *Lives on the Boundary*. Penguin, 1989. One of the most influential
books of my career, it focuses on how schools look to and work for society's
overlooked, failed communities, based in part on stories from Rose's own
life history.

Richard Sennett and Jonathan Cobbs. *The Hidden Injuries of Class*. Vintage, 1973.
The best book I know of (plus Mike Rose's) on what and how class works to
undermine student achievement, and much else besides.

Charles E. Silberman. *Crisis in the Classroom*. Vintage, 1970. This book had a profound impact on my generation of classroom "reformers"—including teachers. It's uncanny to reread the chapter on school reform.

Frank Smith. *Joining the Literacy Club*. Heinemann, 1988. Also *The Book of Learning and Forgetting* (1998). I quote or paraphrase Smith in everything I write
or say; he's so much part of my own thinking now that I often forget to give
credit. These are just two of many worth reading.

Janie Victoria Ward. *The Skin We're In*. Free Press, 2000. A powerful and practical
account that spans the past several generations with both analysis and description useful above all to families—but by extension to schools as well—
on growing up strong, smart, and black.

Lillian Weber. *Looking Back and Thinking Forward*. Teachers College Press, 1997. A
voice that influenced many of today's school-based reformers; passionate and
precise. I am one among many who especially miss her voice today.

Etienne Weiger. *Communities of Practice: Learning, Meaning, and Identity*. Cambridge University Press, 1998. Fascinating, even if at times an academic effort
to explain an approach to teaching and learning that overlaps with the argument of this book, although largely based on nonschool situations.

V. The Context—The Social and Political

Benjamin Barber. *A Passion for Democracy*. Princeton University Press, 1998. If
schools serve democratic purposes, we need a lot of thinking about what it is
about democracy that needs passing on. Barber's take on this was useful as I
thought about schools.

Isaiah Berlin. *Against the Current*. Viking Press, 1980. I read Berlin for many
reasons beyond the connections I find to issues of education. This particular book is also the source for my favorite quote on the misuse of science and mathematical precision in domains they don't (at least yet) belong in.

Harry Boyte. *The Community Is Possible.* Harper & Row, 1984. One of many books by Boyte, who buoys my spirits whenever I think it may not be possible. Based on his experiences building political skills among young and old people in nonschool settings.

Geoffrey Canada. *Fist, Stick, Knife, Gun.* Beacon, 1995. An important account of what it means to grow up in many of our urban communities—yesterday and today—and how critical relationships are to negotiating a safe passage.

Michael Harrington. *The War on Poverty* (Holt, 1984) and *The Long-Distance Runner* (Universal, 1991). As I look back on my life this early political mentor of mine provides a reminder of the connections I found between a way of seeing the larger world and the way of seeing our school worlds.

Christopher Jencks. "Who Should Control Education?" *Dissent Magazine,* March–April 1966. Written in the midst of another era, it predicts with eerie accuracy what was about to happen, and its thoughts about solutions reads well nearly forty years later.

Robert Kuttner. *Everything for Sale.* Knopf, 1997. A good read for understanding the risks to children of an unfettered market ideology by one of our best and sanest economists.

Sarah Lawrence-Lightfoot. *Respect.* Perseus Books, 2000. Although not focused on schools (only one of the subsections is directly about teaching) it is all about how trust and respect connect.

Laura Pappano. *The Connection Gap.* Rutgers, 2001. Together with Robert Putnam's *Bowling Alone* (Touchtone, 2001) made me feel that my alarm over the company kids aren't keeping is not just in my imagination.

Robert B. Reich. *The Future of Success.* Knopf, 2001. The world the kids are entering is laid before us, by someone with my own inclinations, and needs to be kept in mind when we talk about their schooling.

Michael Walzer. "Thoughts on Democratic Schools." *Dissent Magazine,* Winter 1976. A wise piece on the pluses and minuses of different approaches to school governance—worth rereading today.

ACKNOWLEDGMENTS

This book went to the publisher just a month after the World Trade Center attack and a few weeks after the Congress of the United States decided we were at war. It thus was written without those events in mind. My unsettled dis-ease with much of what is happening, my lack of clear resolution with regard to what we should or shouldn't be doing worldwide, made finishing the book itself seem an anticlimax—but in its way maybe even more relevant. Daily life at school helped me—the children's needs for routine kept me moving forward. My hopefulness was sorely tried during the days when I was completing this book, but my sense of the importance of the topic of this book —can and should children be raised in settings of trust—was, if anything, enhanced by the events of September 11.

Various chapters in the book have benefited from the criticism of friends—my especial thanks to readers Brenda Engel, Robert Fried, Emily Gasoi, Heidi Lyne, Mike Rose, and Ted Sizer, and also to Walt Haney and Robert Stake for their close reading of the sections on testing (about which they had their disagreements as well as agreements). Being a friend/critic is not easy work.

My editor, Andy Hrycyna, had a hard time getting me to stop tinkering. His patience, suggestions, reactions, and prodding for clarity were invaluable. He is just the editor I needed, and his good editorial ear and willingness to tell me "stop! enough!" was much appreciated. He entered into arguments with me to help me hone my own, but also because he enjoys lively and even heated conversation and takes arguments—and schools—seriously. I'm indebted too for the final editing by Mary Ray Worley—who combed page after page for technical and grammatical errors, but whose concern for the sense of things was even more invaluable. Thanks also to Milly Marmur for holding my hand, giving advice, and being a friend, as well as my agent.

A lifetime of enjoying arguments has made me an oddball in the world of schooling, but has also had its bonuses. I didn't give my father, Joseph Willen, a lot of credit in my first book, but he was the model of the arguer as irritant, to whom I am—when all is said and done—very grateful. Now that there is once again a Joseph Willen (under the age of two) in the family, I am reminded of how much the first one influenced me. My mother, Pearl Willen, and my brother, Paul Willen, have been the usual beneficiaries of my public appreciation—the latter more and more as we grow older. But Joe was—for better and at times, my friends will tell you, for the worse—the model.

Both my daughter, Becky, and son Nick have been invaluable sources of stories, which sometimes require me to revisit one of my grander theories when it doesn't fit their experiences as teachers in schools in western Massachusetts and California. Roger and Tricia keep me filled with the travails of educating kids in New York's public schools (they've tried quite a few as parents); and all three of my kids remind me on occasion of the mistakes I made in educating them. But all three have most of all been kind personal allies. My grandchildren—Sarah, Ezra, Daniel, and Lilli—have had lots to say, in passing, on the subjects this book deals with, and they are the ultimate advisors I turn to when I want to check on my own firsthand impressions of what matters. Thanks also go to Fred Meier for patiently listening, mostly without comment, as I struggled through this manuscript.

Of course, this particular book is, above all, the outgrowth of five years in the company of a particular group of people—those connected with Mission Hill School in Boston. I took on the task of starting a new school in part because of the pleasure it gave me to be able to work more closely with several old friends and colleagues: Vito Perrone, Brenda Engel, Eleanor Duckworth, Linda Nathan, Dennis Littky, and Ted Sizer—each an educator of extraordinary talent. It was the result of an inspired thought driving to Boston without my radio—"what shall I do with the rest of my life?" The answer brought immediate joy: give up being a wise retired consultant and go back inside a school. I have not been disappointed. It led also to relationships with a whole host of new people. I can never sufficiently repay the debt I owe to Dawn Lewis, who in the midst of her own professional and personal crises—starting a school and moving to Europe—held my hand as I ordered furniture and supplies, hired staff, and so on. There were the members of the founding committee—who met with me to give advice, provide support and more: Sandra Alvarado, Claryce Evans, Allen Graubard (who drafted the original proposal), Robin Harris, Lady June Hubbard, Beth Lerman, Dawn Lewis, David Perrigo, Anna Perry, Jackie Rivers, and Beatriz Zapatar, as well as Vito, Eleanor, Linda, and Brenda.

The staff, kids, and families of the Mission Hill School—from full-timers to part-timers—are the major actors in the stories in this book. Although I have shared chapters along the way with the faculty, they bear no responsibility for its errors, its viewpoint, its truths and half-truths. (See their names listed separately.) Of course, my deepest thanks to them all.

This whole Boston venture would have been impossible had the superintendent, Tom Payzant, not wanted it to happen (and despite frequent differences of opinion about this or that, stuck to the agreement that wooed me to Boston), had the Boston Teachers Union under the leadership of Ed Doherty not pushed for, and steadfastly lived up to, an unusual contract that gave ten schools freedom and autonomy from city and union rules, and had not Linda Nathan and Larry Myatt established a support network of schools connected through the Center for Collaborative Education under the leadership of Dan French. Then there was Albee Holland's guidance in helping us deal with the Boston Public School bureaucracy—indefatigable and indispensable. As editor of our weekly Mission Hill newsletter, Ed Miller has been a careful reader of whatever I'm writing—and he's played devil's advocate when needed. Thanks also to Dave Perrigo, Heidi Foster, and the staff and students of the New Mission High School, who share 67 Alleghany Street with us, for being good friends and 98 percent of the time perfect cotenants.

The financial generosity of a number of individuals and foundations also helped make my own life feasible, so that undertaking this seemed less unreasonable, as well as making Mission Hill School stronger. In particular, thanks to Mrs. Walter Annenberg, Lucille Hayes, Terri and Eve Herndon, Pam Solo, Sherman Wolfe, and the Bill and Melinda Gates Foundation. (Thanks also to David Ferraro of the Gates Foundation for the St. Augustine quote!)

Special thanks, in a category that has no equivalent, to Helen Fouhey, who has played a very special role in my life. Helen has been a sort of private and invaluable think tank for me—since the school began—along with all the other hats she wears in making Mission Hill work.

Finally, there are all my New York friends and longtime colleagues, whom I can't ever get out of my mind and heart. I ache over every setback and cheer every victory as I follow each and every one of the many schools I've been connected with over the years. I read Jane Andrias and Sid Massey's weekly newsletters from Central Park East and River East, and I plagiarize liberally. I follow Paul Schwarz's new venture at Landmark, Ann Cook's tireless work both at the Urban Academy and on a statewide level to keep the fires burning. Then there continue to be those many phone calls, e-mails, and visits with Cece Cunningham, Alan Dichter, Sherry King, Bruce Kanze, Nancy Mann, Nancy Mohr, Marion Mogolescu, Eric Nadelstern, Sylvia Rabiner, and Peter Steinberg to conspire together to improve the world. They also help me remember how much we've permanently changed New York, city and state. I run into graduates of Central Park East and Central Park East Secondary School in the oddest places—on bikes along Huntington Avenue in Boston, airport lobbies in Chicago, meetings in Providence—and then there are the not-infrequent phone calls. As I write this, I have just returned from an event in New York City organized by Central Park East Secondary School graduates that reminded me of how much these kinds of schools can act as ballast in a tough and sometimes tragically out-of-whack world. To all my New York City colleagues, thank you, but a very special thank you to Jane Andrias for keeping the dream alive in the deepest sense. While many years my junior, she has become a mentor of sorts, keeping me intellectually and spiritually on my toes as I watch what the first Central Park East has grown into so many years later.

Who's Who at Mission Hill School

We began in the summer of 1997 with the following lean staff: Emily Gasoi, Alicia Carroll, Heidi Lyne, Angel Alonso, Geralyn Bywater, Marla Gaines-Harris, Brian Straughter, and volunteers Brenda Engel and Beth Lerman, plus classroom interns, and lunchroom helpers Sharon Taylor and Monica Diaz, who also tirelessly managed security and the buses the first two years, and current art teacher Jeanne Rachko, who started with us as a classroom assistant. James McGovern joined the staff in January 1998, when Angel left teaching to return to the world of publishing. Sharon left at the end of year one, Monica in fall 1999, Beth in fall 2000, and Emily moved to Paris in fall 2001. Everyone else is still with us.

By the fall of 2001, the classroom teaching staff also included, in order of appearance: Kathy Clunis, Ayla Gavins, Alphonse Litz, Emily Chang, Roberta Logan, Matthew Knoester, and Jenerra Williams. The full-time staff included Thomas Archer, Lukas Best (who goes back to year one), Helen Fouhey, Carla Johnson, Karen Krisiukenas-Bennett, Amina Michele-Lord, Jon Ouckama, John McSweeney, and John Wolfe, who nearly twenty years after we worked together at Central Park East II joined us in Boston. Finally, we've thrived because of full-timers Paul Nowacki and John Walsh, our extraordinary custodians, as well as Sylvia Britto, the manager of our cafeteria, who seeks always to wheedle a little more and better food out of the Boston public schools.

We were joined also by an increasing number of regular part-timers, some paid and some not: Deborah Baye, Ilene Carver, Minna Choi, Delores Costello, Kelly Jean Freeman, Robert Fried, Edna Handy, Kevin Harris, Jo-Ann Hawkesworth, Ed Miller, Mirian Rubinow, Ann Ruggiero, Gabe Shapiro, Polly Wagner, Veronica Zepeda, and folks from the College of Pharmacology, and many other institutions and individuals who support our work—providing expertise, educational services, and financial aid.

Not least are those vital one-year (or one-semester) interns from Harvard, Northeastern, Lesley, and Tufts, who will soon enough be great teachers themselves.

Vito Perrone was our first board chair, Mitch Hilton followed him, and Bruce Smith now serves in that post, along with a rotating governing board consisting of an equal number of parents and staff, an esteemed group of community leaders, and two students.

Each year key parents take leading roles. If we include all those who volunteer in one way or another, the list is almost as long as the list of families we serve and longer than the staff. We would have no library or after-school program, for example, without them. The families of Mission Hill are—as well as our students' first and primary teachers and advocates—critical to the work of Mission Hill.

And a final mention to my first two student advisees—2001 graduate Akwasi Agyemang and graduate-to-be Marika Blue—whose regular lunch dates at Mississippi's gave me heart and knowledge.